Take A Hike

Exploring Ontario Trails
Vol. 1

Fay Beck-Ryall

with Foreword by **Michael B. Davie**

Manor House Publishing Inc.

National Library of Canada
Cataloguing in Publication:

Beck-Ryall, Fay,
Take A Hike

Beck-Ryall, Fay
Exploring Ontario trails / Fay Beck-Ryall:
edited with a foreword by Michael B. Davie.

(Take A Hike : v. 1)

ISBN: 978-1-897453-25-4

1. Hiking—Ontario—Guidebooks.
2. Trails—Ontario—Guidebooks.
3. Ontario—Guidebooks.
I. Davie, Michael B. II. Title. III. Series.

GV199.44C22058 2003   796.51'09713   C2003-906009-8

Copyright 2003-10-15
By Fay Beck-Ryall.
Editors: Michael B. Davie, Kim Arnott
Includes Index, photography
Published November 15, 2003
by Manor House Publishing: (905) 648-2193
www.manor-house.biz.

First edition.   All rights reserved.
Cover photo; photography throughout: Fay Beck-Ryall
Cover Design: Fay Beck-Ryall/Michael B. Davie.
The publisher gratefully acknowledges the financial
support of the Book Publishing Industry Development
Program (BPIDP), Department of Canadian Heritage.

Manor House Publishing
(905) 648-2193

Dedication:

To my husband and supportive hiking partner Norm,

And, to my children,
Nancy Jaffray and Darrell Beck

"My true success has been my children."

Acknowledgements:

Special thanks go out to the Hamilton Spectator for giving me the opportunity to write a weekly hiking column, which in turn allowed me to pursue, through my readers and friends, the need for this book.

Also, to my editor Kim Arnott, Professional Member of the Periodical Writers Association of Canada, I extend my heartfelt appreciation for her kindness and professional ability when it came to editing my work.

To Michael B. Davie and Manor House Publishing, many thanks for taking a chance on this writer and making my first book a reality.

To my husband who was always ready to take a hike. Thank you.
And to my children who trusted our hiking abilities and never seemed to worry about our safe return. Through hasty notes on the kitchen table, they always knew the area where we were hiking.

- Fay Beck-Ryall.

Foreword

Take a hike! – it's an attention-getting phrase that marks a refreshing change from staid let's-enjoy-nature books of the past. And that's entirely appropriate.

After all, reading about enjoying nature should itself be an enjoyable experience, expressed in plain English in an interesting, compelling manner.

Fay Beck-Ryall does just that: Based on her popular hiking column in The Hamilton Spectator, her first-ever book, Take A Hike, is a practical, down-to-earth guide for enjoying hiking experiences throughout South Central Ontario.

The author not only leads you along some truly intriguing trails, she also describes in detail, some of the scenic views, joys and pitfalls you may encounter along the way.

Fay Beck-Ryall leads off with her own first hiking experience, an experience that provided the impetus for writing this book: She wanted to read a book outlining some of the Hamilton-Halton-Niagara area hiking trails, including information on how to get to these sites, how long it would normally take to complete a given hike, the level of difficulty/expertise involved, things to watch out for, helpful tips, and some of the sights and sounds one might encounter.

She discovered no such hiking books exist for the local South Central Ontario area. So, she put pen to paper and wrote one herself. The result is an exciting, interesting, easy-to-follow, in-depth look at the hidden delights that await on some outstanding local trails.

The author's engaging writing style will also have you snickering sympathetically as she relates hikes that did not go smoothly – all part of a learning experience.

So let's join Fay on the trail – and Take A Hike!

- Michael B. Davie.

About the author

As a child, freelance writer and photographer Fay Beck-Ryall learned to love nature through the early teachings of her Grandfather. These teachings led to a life-long interest in backpack hiking. She has been writing about hiking Ontario's trails since 1999.

Fay's deep appreciation of the beauty and wonderment of the natural world all around us is skilfully reflected in her writing and photography.

Fay has been a successful freelance writer since 1999, working as a newspaper columnist, interviewer/reporter, and writer for magazines such as Airborne, Canadian Gardening, and Inflight.

The versatile writer is equally at home with fiction, non-fiction and documentaries, and has a natural eye for spectacular outdoor photography.

Fay resides in Waterdown, Ontario, where she enjoys the outdoors and continues to expand her success as a writer and photographer. She is also a professional member of the Periodical Writers Association of Canada.

Contents/Index of hikes:

Trail and month of hike:

1. Dundas Valley/Spring Creek Trail (March)
2. Spencer Gorge (April)
3. North Shore, Royal Botanical Gardens (April)
4. Christie Round the Lake (April)
5. Beamer Trail (April)
6. App's Mill Nature Trail (April)
7. DeCew Falls (April)
8. Woodend Conservation. Area & Bruce Trail (April)
9. Tiffany & Sherman Falls (May)
10. Crawford Lake Trails (May)
11. Red Hill Valley (May)
12. Dundas Valley – headwaters trail (May)
13. Dundas Valley – Main Loop (May)
14. Valens Conservation Area (June)
15. Westfield Woods (June)
16. Crook's Hollow (July)
17. Chippewa Creek Trail (July)
18. St. John's Sassafras Stroll (July)
19. Bruce Trail at Smokey Hollow (July)
20. F.W.R. Dickson Wilderness Trail (July)
21. Paris to Cambridge Rail Trail (August)
22. Hilton Falls (August)
23. Buffalo Craig Trail/Vista Adventure (August)
24. Bruce Trail at Kern's Rd. (August)
25. Mountsberg Lakeshore Lookout (September)
26. Backus Heritage Trail (September)
27. Black Creek Side Trail (September)
28. Devil's Punch Bowl (September)
29. River and Ruin/Bruce Link (October)
30. Webster's Falls (October)
31. Borer's Falls (October)
32. Ball's Falls (November)
33. Mount Nemo (November)
34. Twenty-Mile Creek (November)
35. Felker's Falls on Red Hill Creek (November)
36. Fay's Five Favourites

Introduction:
Fay's First Hike

I guess turning 50 for some of us is a natural progression into happiness and contentment, but for others it means taking a new path into the unknown, leaving behind everything that made you who you are.

While you are pondering over which path to take, you find yourself wrestling with the steering wheel, while spinning your tires trying to get back onto the familiar road you have traveled all your life.

You're like a leaf in the wind, fluttering here and there, disconnected and free, not knowing where you are going to land. The children have already left, or are just on the threshold and after 20 years everyone expects you to stop being a parent.

You talk too little, or too much. Words you have said in the past all of a sudden become unimportant, or horribly wrong. Overnight, you have become a transparent piece of the furniture. You feel your life is sand, slowly running through an hourglass, and your afraid that what remains of your life will feel like an hour. You wake up one morning and realize that you and your partner have really not much in common, except for one thing – the Great Outdoors!

I've always been a walker, but a couple of years ago I suggested to my husband we take up backpack hiking. He had no qualms about giving it a try, so we excitedly researched and purchased some equipment. The most important part of the body when hiking is the feet. Good hiking boots are a must. To get a real feel for this new spring adventure, we packed a lunch, brought along the camera and binoculars and hiked some flat terrain mulch-covered paths only a few miles from our home. Soon it was summer vacation and both of us were looking for something new, an adventure.

We packed our newly-bought hiking equipment, loaded our new pickup truck and struck out for a three day hiking trip in Northern Ontario! Being as green as grass, little did we know that we were heading into the most rugged trails imaginable, at the very end of the Bruce Trail, at Tobermory.

It was a cool cloudy day as we pulled into the parking lot of the motel that served as our base camp. We stepped out of the truck and got our first gulp of the cool summer breeze drifting across the lake. A couple of sailboats and a fishing trawler drifted into the harbour on the clearest blue water, I've ever seen.

This is going to be great, I thought, as I shivered and quickly turned the key. We threw our equipment on the bed and went to our window to view the lake.

Since, it was already late in the day, we decided to eat our packed lunch and take a short hike into the village, nestled around the harbour. We'd map out the trails. Tomorrow would be our first full day of hiking.

We awoke early, quickly showered and dressed and enjoyed a continental breakfast in the motel restaurant overlooking the lake. To get to the starting point of our first trail, we had to drive a few miles south and then turn east into a parking lot.

A sign indicated bears were often in the area, but my husband convinced me it was probably a warning, not reality, when I initially refused to leave the truck.

Our map marked a six-mile loop that would take us out to rocky cliffs and a panoramic view of the lake.

Our backpacks were much heavier than the light loads we were used to for treks around home. They were filled with everything from rain gear, food for the day or overnight if needed, bug spray, flashlight, emergency kit, and warm clothes. To my husband's dismay, I was prepared for the worst-case scenario.

Although, our map information gave directions, there was no notice on how difficult the trail might be; beginner, intermediate or advanced. It began as a beginner trail, with a crushed stone path, well marked, and well traveled by other human beings. This is great, we thought, a piece of cake.

But soon, it turned to an intermediate trail and we were beginning to wonder if we had taken on more of a challenge than we had planned. We crossed a wooden bridge and not wanting to admit we were inexperienced wimps, we began a narrow trail through thick forest, green slime, deep crevices, twisted tree roots and big slippery boulders as far as the eye could see.

Each step took us farther into difficult terrain that to this day we haven't encountered anywhere else. Focusing on every step as not to turn an ankle or lose our footing, we often had to stop and make sure we were still on the trail. Not another human being in sight, and thank heavens, no bears. Besides, no one or anything would be stupid enough to be out here in the middle of nowhere, and heaven forbid if we had to run from a bear. Tree climbing was not my thing.

We were maintaining a slow pace, but determined to reach our destination. Time was passing quickly and we didn't want to try to navigate this trail in the dark it would have been virtually impossible. Thoughts of camping overnight began to haunt me. After hours of constant climbing and concentration, we came to the lake and trail markings leading us across a vast outlay of round, white rocks, each the size of a coffee mug.

None of the rocks were stable and they rolled with every step. I stopped, exhausted, and ready to give up.

Finally, we came to a road that seemed to be heading nowhere. No loop, no signs, only a log to rest on and eat some of our lunch. We had no idea where we were and we hadn't seen another human being since we left the motel.

We had a decision to make, to either follow the road and hope it came out onto a highway, or return the same way we came.

We knew the trail back didn't excite us much, but at least we were confident that it would take us back to our truck. The road idea was an unknown. Really tired now, we gathered up our stuff and headed back.

Our first hike was far more frightening and challenging than anyone could ever imagine, but it paved the way for our continuing interest in hiking and a brand new appreciation of the dangers and the beauty of nature.

Needed Equipment:

Hiking can be the most inexpensive of all sports.

You will spend the most money on a good pair of properly fitted, laced, high-top hiking boots.

You will not regret the cost, as comfort and safety should be your top priority.

Carry your own backpack, and stock it with plenty of water, food (in an insulated lunch bag with a small freezer pack), a first aid kit, insect repellent, tissues, a pocket knife, flashlight, a whistle (if you need to call for help), a rain poncho, a map of the trail (helpful, as trails are not always clearly marked), a camera and binoculars, if you wish.

Take along anything else you think you might need, but remember.....you are carrying it. Encourage the kids to carry their own backpacks with food, water and a whistle.

Helpful Hints:

Do not go off the trail. You would not believe how quickly you can become disoriented if you don't stay on the trail.

There will be colored circles or strips of paint on trees along the route. Follow the markings and be aware of what is around you. On advanced trails, you concentrate on every step, so take the time to stop and look around. You do not want to miss a spectacular view, a flower, or peculiar rock formation or tree.

With everyone carrying their own backpack of supplies, it ensures that if anyone should get separated from the group (heaven forbid), their supplies will sustain them until they are found. Carry a watch and check the time as you first begin the trail. Since you really do not know how long it will take you to complete the hike, check the time periodically and recognize that it will take you that much time to return.

Unless you are hiking in an isolated area, you will meet other hikers along the way who are friendly and willing to help. All of the trails I will be profiling are not always well traveled and washroom facilities are an added bonus, so there may be times when the nearest tree or bush may suffice.

Dress for the weather and layer clothing. As you walk you may get overheated and wish to shed that jacket. Do not wear cologne. Bugs love it! Mosquitoes are attracted to dark coloured clothing, so wear light colours, long sleeves and pants. For added protection make sure you apply bug repellent.

We found early morning is the most comfortable time to hit the trails. The air is fresh and cool. It also provides you with the full light of day for your return, if you happen to get lost or have taken the wrong turn.

So, come on ... let's **Take a Hike**.

Sulphur Springs Station

1.
Dundas Valley Conservation Area Spring Creek Trail

Difficulty: Beginner to intermediate
Directions: From 403, take Hwy. 52 to Copetown. Turn right on Governor's Rd. (Regional Rd. 299) to the main entrance of the Dundas Conservation Area. There is an admission fee.

It had rained the day before and we knew late March was a bit early to hit the trails. But the southeasterly breeze had a hint of warmth in it and the blue sky promised spring had finally arrived.

We had been to the Dundas Valley Conservation area last year when we hiked the Main Loop Trail, and got lost when we took a wrong turn, an embarrassing moment I won't mention too often. So, make sure you get a map of the area at the Visitor Center.

The Visitor Center, a reproduction of a Victorian Railway Station, is about a five-minute, easy walk from the parking lot, and it is here where all the other trails branch off.

Today, we decided to take the Spring Creek Trail. It winds northeast off into the forest and in a few minutes you will arrive at an information board with instructions on warm-up exercises.

If you feel fit enough to attempt the fitness trail, it loops off to the right of the main path and then farther down, connects back. There are obstacle structures built along the main trail if you wish to test your fitness level. We decided we didn't want to know.

We checked the time and began our hike.

Hard-packed earth and gravel made up the trail surface with some small uphill grades, but it was a pleasant walk with the creek almost always in view. In low-lying areas it became quite wet and muddy, but not impassable.

We were glad we were wearing a good pair of waterproof hiking boots. Make it a practice to keep other shoes in your vehicle for your return. You may want to get out of those hot, sometimes muddy boots.

Since it was still too early for the leaves to have formed on the trees, we could clearly see the creek widen and narrow with an array of currents pushing through the foliage creating tiny waterfalls as the water cascaded over fallen logs. It's a path it has followed for hundreds of years.

Just where the trail bordered the creek bank, I noticed across the widest portion, nestled into the grass, tiny spots of yellow. Could be wild flowers I thought, but it was too far away to tell.

We pushed on, down some hills, over a bridge where a mallard duck with his mate were swimming casually along the creek, periodically diving under the water for food. Oh, the male was so beautiful with his green and white markings beside the drab brown female. They didn't like us invading their privacy, so they slowly turned away and headed back up stream.

Enjoying what seemed like a moderate walking pace, we had become quite warm as we came to the end of the Spring Creek Trail, so we removed our jackets, stopped for lunch and checked the time. It had been an hour, so it would be an hour back, as this trail does not loop your return the same way you came. I thought retracing our steps would be a bit boring, but it is remarkable how many sights are overlooked and missed entirely when you pass by the first time.

As we began our trek back, poking through the grass at the trails edge, were yellow spring flowers called Coltsfoot. It's a dandelion-like plant with a flower head about one inch and thin spiky petals surrounding the centre. It blooms from February to June and it got its name from the leaf, which is supposed to resemble a colt's foot. According to the Field Guide to North American Wildflowers, the extract from the fresh leaves can be used for making cough drops or hard candy, and its dried leaves can be steeped for tea. So don't step on the Coltsfoot.

Farther on, we crossed paths again with the mallard duck and his mate, swimming upstream in rhythm, as graceful as a dance in slow motion.

Creeping as quietly as I could, I reach the edge of the creek and knelt down behind a fallen log to get a photo. Realizing I was there, they just paddled away, unruffled, determined to complete their mission.

Our return hike did give a new perspective: Views from different angles, a variety of tree formations we hadn't seen before and hills that had somehow grown steeper. It hadn't occurred to us that the opening trail had been a gentle downhill walk. But coming back it was a continuous uphill climb, some grades steeper than others.

Even if you think you are reasonably fit, as we do, the added weight of your backpack and heavier boots all add to the workout resistance.

Hearts pumping and getting a little tired now, our last leg of the hike and the parking lot was in full view.

Our hiking time had been two hours and fifteen minutes. It had been a good workout, and a very pleasant experience for the first hike of the season.

Spencer Gorge Falls

2.
Spencer Gorge Waterfalls Trail

Difficulty: Intermediate and advanced
Directions: Take Hwy. 8 from Dundas, turn right on Brock Rd. and right at the flashing light onto Harvest Rd. Turn right onto Short Rd. and left onto Fallsview Rd. This is the first parking lot, and closest to Webster's Falls and picnic area. Further down Harvest Road is the second parking lot, which is closest to the Tews Falls trail and Dundas Peak lookout. When we were there, a parking fee was required at either lot.

Spencer Gorge Waterfalls Trail at Greensville is one of most spectacular walking trails that we have so far discovered.

Tews Falls trail provides a view of the falls, which plunge 41 metres (134.5 feet), compared to the Horseshoe Falls in Niagara at 52 metres (171 feet).

The trail leads out to Dundas Peak, revealing a breath-taking vista overlooking Dundas Valley. The wide width of the gorge downstream suggests that at one time these falls handled as much water volume as the more famous Horseshoe Falls in Niagara.

This is a trail that is not so well traveled. As it loops back, it takes you away from the edge of the escarpment and brings you out to the parking lot area. From there you can follow the Bruce Trail along the escarpment, which eventually opens up into another parking lot, a large picnic area, and Webster's Falls.

In this area, you can stand at a railing and look down at the cascading torrents of water, or if you are more adventurous, you can descend a number of steep narrow stairs to the base of the falls.

This area, and the picnic area bordering along the fast-flowing Spencer Creek, are yours to discover with just a short, easy walk from the first parking lot.

In late April, we decided to make Tews Falls trail our second hike of the season.

It was a cool, sunny day. The buds on the trees were just beginning to burst, and the trail was dry with hard-packed earth, tree roots, and rocks. Patches of wild violets dotted areas along the path.

A fallen tree trunk, split and dried, still showed signs of life with a number of tiny branches sprouting tiny yellow leaves. To me, it was an example of the power of nature refusing to die. It was spring, and everything was coming to life.

We stood mesmerized by the view at Dundas Peak, made the loop back to the parking lot, and continued on the Bruce Trail to Webster's Falls, where we sat along the rocks on the creek bank, and ate lunch. We then returned by the same route, back to our vehicle.

On these trails there are a number of sets of stairs to climb, so remember, going down is a lot easier than going up.

At an average walking pace, and stopping for pictures and lunch, this hike took us approximately two and a half hours.

3.
Royal Botanical Gardens North Shore Trail

Difficulty: Beginner to Intermediate
Directions: From Hwy 6 south turn right onto York Rd. at the flashing light intersection. Turn left onto Old Guelph Rd. and watch for the Arboretum entrance on your right. From Plains Rd. West /York Blvd. West, turn right on Old Guelph Rd. and watch for the entrance on your right. There is an admission fee.

The North Shore Trail of Cootes Paradise Nature Sanctuary begins at the wetland exhibit building, located just beyond the gates to the Royal Botanical Gardens Arboretum.

This building houses some live exhibits of turtles and fish, along with picture-boards explaining the history of the nature preserve. Here there are an abundance of maps and information that will prove useful on your hike.

As you begin to descend down a steep gravel path you'll pass by an amazing collection of rhododendrons, not yet in bloom, when we were there in early April.

As you reach the water's edge off to your left is a Bee-yard, where as many as 50,000 bees hive and may visit 20 million flowers during the summer.

We took the grass path to the right called, Captain Cootes Trail. This is easy walking and even in early spring, there were many things to see and explore.

A huge flock of Black-Capped Chickadees had gathered around a rotted out log, where someone had left a good supply of birdseed. They startled me a little because I have a fear of birds, generated by a rooster attack as a small child. But these birds were cute and small, I lost my fear in seconds and took some photos.

Another hiker passed by at that moment and he appeared not to have noticed this fascinating scene, so I asked him he had seen the birds.

He was very friendly and stopped to tell me that if I was very still and held out some birdseed, they would come and eat out of my hand. I wasn't that brave.

Just as we were talking, a woodpecker came and perched on a branch within three feet of where we were standing. He had no fear of us, and flitted about, not bothered by the fact that I was talking his picture.

The hiker told me that this species was called "Downy Woodpecker," smallest of all woodpeckers and common throughout Ontario. The males are the only ones with a bright red cap.

There were plenty of other types of birds in the area, including Canada geese. And fun-loving squirrels playfully scampered at our feet as we trekked along Captain Cootes Trail.

It was still too early for wildflowers, but we found many interesting trees. Some, due to old age, had met their demise and had fallen over to rot away and return to the earth.

All along the trail there were footbridges, small streams, and a large marsh area.

Hickory Island provided an astonishing site of lifeless trees bleached white by the sun and dotted with a large colony of birds returning to their nests. To get a closer look, binoculars would be useful.

If you stay on Captain Cootes Trail, a good walking path, it will lead out to Bulls Point Lookout, taking about 45 minutes at a moderate walk from the Nature Center.

At this point you can retrace your steps or take a loop consisting of the Marsh Walk, and Grey Doe Trail, which will eventually take you to Captain Cootes Trail and back to the beginning of your hike.

Because it was so early in the spring, these walks were slippery and muddy. But a little adventure only adds interest to a curious mind.

The Marsh Walk loops off the Captain Cootes Trail and heads down toward the waters' edge, where a long boardwalk leads out to a steel constructed lookout tower that overlooks Rat Island.

Along the sides of the boardwalk there are no railings, but it is very well-constructed and makes for easy walking.

Upon leaving, veer to the left and return to the trail as it winds upward back to the Captain Cootes Trail. From the top of the trail turn a bit to the right and there you will see a sign for the Grey Doe Trail. This trail is uphill, more challenging and rugged and at this time of year, extremely slippery with mud.

As the Grey Doe Trail joins back to the Captain Cootes, there's a bridge and a small waterfall providing a pleasant and relaxing sound of a gentle flowing stream. Our return trip back to the Nature Center took us past the gathering of chickadees still coming to feed at the old tree stump. The loop of the three trails took us about two hours to complete.

We'll revisit this trail in May when lilacs are in bloom. As with most trails, there are rules to preserve nature. Posted signs advise keeping to the pedestrian trail and keeping dogs on a leash. Removing plants is forbidden. No motorized boats or vehicles are allowed in the Sanctuary, and there's no cycling on trails.

Christie Conservation picnic area

4.
Christie Conservation Area
Around the Lake

Difficulty: Beginner (Good for families with children)
Directions: From Hwy. 401 take Hwy. 6 South and turn right, (west) on Hwy. 5. From Hwy. 403 take Hwy. 6, North, and turn left, on Hwy. 5. The large Christie Conservation sign and entrance is on your left, and is about a15 minute drive from Hwy. 6. There is an admission fee for a day pass.

    The months of July and August are probably the best times to explore this conservation area.
    But if you are looking for a scenic hike, this is not the place to go. The main attraction here is a beautiful supervised beach and vast expanse of picnic area.
    There is a large building with a concession stand for snacks, washroom facilities and change rooms.
    Beautifully landscaped and maintained, this picnic area has all the comforts for a great day at the beach.
    The lake is a calm 151 acres, ideal for canoes, which can be rented on the property.
    After a swim and a picnic lunch, it would be an ideal time to take that walk around the lake.
    Going west along the beach, you will come to a cofferdam, which divides the main lake, and a series of stocked trout ponds near Middletown Road.

Turning left on the trail closest to the lake, you will begin your walk through the woods.

When we were there in early April it was still too soon for the spring flowers to emerge, but their leaves were beginning to appear through winter's refuge of dead grass and leaves. The trail is not scenic, and only a periodic glimpse of the lake is barely visible from the path. The wild shrubs grow high, creating a dense undergrowth of twisted vines and branches, blocking out the view of the lake and wide expanse of beach.

Be careful here, as there are small trails branching off to the water's edge that lead nowhere. Stick to the trail that seems most traveled.

The footing is hard-packed earth and grass, with rolling hills and steep slopes.

Along the way are a variety of green ferns, and a soft carpet of pine needles. This trail links to the Wedelin Run, Lowland and Wilderness Trails. These trails are identified with names and symbols written on wooden posts.

It is about a 30 to 45 minute walk, which leads you to the 30-foot high Christie Dam, with a perfect view of the lake.

As you cross the dam and turn back west, a short walk will bring you back to the beach and picnic area.

5.
Beamer Trail

Difficulty: Beginner to Intermediate
Directions: From the Burlington Skyway Bridge, Niagara bound, take exit 71 (Christie Street exit). Continue south and turn right on Ridge Road West and right onto Quarry Road and follow the conservation signs. From the Skyway Bridge to Beamer's Falls on Ridge Road takes about 20 minutes. There's no entry fee but donations are welcome.

The Beamer Memorial Conservation Area, near Grimsby, with a side link to the Bruce Trail, will always be one of our most memorable experiences.

It is a magnificent sight in springtime, as the water thunders and tumbles over rocks of the Forty Mile Creek far below, and it was at its peak water capacity when we arrived in mid-April.

Travelling on Ridge Road West, before you get to the Conservation entrance, you will see a large cement bridge. Park in a small area, just before the bridge. On your right is Beamer's Falls.

There is a very steep incline down to the base of the falls that is extremely dangerous, so proceed at your own risk.

Clinging to small trees for support and testing for loose rock, I made my way down to the base of the falls. Despite the risk, I had to get those photographs.

Beamer Falls

Be sure to watch children and pets along the top ridge, as there are no railings. This applies to most of the hiking trails.

At the beginning of the Beamer Trail, there is an open field with a lookout tower to watch the spring hawk migration, washroom facilities, boards with interesting facts about the trail, and a map.

This trail is wheelchair accessible out to the first lookout, with a spectacular view of Grimsby, Lake Ontario, and the shorelines of Burlington and Toronto.

The remainder of the trail is flat, easy walking with hard packed earth, tree roots and rocks. Along this route there are two other lookouts and the last one will give you a birds eye view of the Forty Mile Creek far below on the valley floor. Just past the third and last lookout you will come to the link to the Bruce Trail on your left. I strongly suggest that if you are somewhat adventurous, this trail is a must.

The Bruce Trail begins with a number of steps constructed of wooden sections dug into the earth and leads you down to a hard packed trail that runs along the Forty Mile Creek. Here, hidden in the valley, we discovered the most picturesque views of waterfalls and fast water that we have ever seen.

The morning sunlight filtering through the trees cast shadows and bright light on huge rock formations, some covered in green moss, highlighting the raging water that churned up foam by the thundering cascades of water as it twisted and turned in a spellbinding vista that most of us only see in movies.

Every turn, every new sight seemed better than the first, as we traveled along the Bruce Trail. The desire to capture this on film was overwhelming, but still-film doesn't carry the sounds and feelings of the moment – those you must remember.

To our left we could look up hundreds of feet to the top of the ridge where gigantic boulders had slipped away through many years of erosion, and see trees fighting to survive with some of their roots open to the elements. Some of these white cedars are several hundreds of years old. It was still too early for spring flowers, but there were patches of flower leaves getting ready to push their blooms into the sunlight.

The Bruce Trail is well maintained and preserved by the many volunteers of the Bruce Trail Association and follows the creek until you enter the Town of Grimsby and beyond. There, we turned, sat on a huge flat rock overlooking one of the waterfalls and enjoyed our lunch. Reluctantly, we left it all behind and retraced the steady upward climb to Beamer Trail, and hiked the original loop back to the parking area.

If you continue along the escarpment edge instead of making the loop, you'll return to Beamer's Falls and the cement bridge on Ridge Road. Although one of the Beamer Trail highlights is the spring hawk and raptor migration, we only saw a couple of hawks that day. Perhaps it was too early or too late in the season, or it was the wrong time of day, but we were not the only ones disappointed. Positioned at the lookouts were many people with binoculars trained at the sky, hoping to track those magnificent birds as they floated and soared high above the treetops.

According to the Niagara Peninsula Hawkwatch, the best time to see birds is usually between 10 am and 3 pm, from mid-March to mid-May. During this time period an average of 14,500 birds may be seen. But if poor weather has occurred in the south, there will be days when few or no birds are seen.

The Beamer Trail and the Bruce Trail side link took us approximately two hours. Remember, I only give you the times it has taken us. If you walk fast and don't stop long to explore, take pictures or take in the views, it would take less time.

6.
App's Mill Nature Trail

Difficulty: Beginner
Directions: From 403 turn south at Rest Acres Rd. exit, near Brantford. Turn right on Robinson Rd. You will see the sign for the conservation entrance on your left. There is no admission fee.

It was unusually hot for mid-April and visions of wild flowers hung in my mind as we made the 30-minute drive west from Hamilton to the App's Mill Conservation Area, near Brantford.

The Trail begins at the Nature Center, where during the week it is being used for children's classes, but is open to the public on weekends.

There are washroom facilities, facts of history, picnic tables, and plenty of room for children to play. The trail strikes off to the north-west, over an arched wooden and steel bridge that spans Whiteman's Creek, but turns and heads due north toward the mill.

At this time of year the creek had a fast flowing current with a large volume of water.

From the Nature Center to the Mill is wheelchair assessable and about a 10-minute walk. The flour and gristmill is a large building, now dark and abandoned, but looming among the trees statuesque and proud. It was built in 1846 and was reportedly one of the first to export wheat overseas.

As we rounded the building, heading westward, frogs with their loud spring time serenade greeted us from beneath the water foliage growing on the surface of the millpond, but suddenly they fell silent, as we approached. Even tiny minnows knew we were there and swam under a moss-covered branch, hidden, except for their tails swaying in the water current.

Because this is a cold-water creek, brook, brown and rainbow trout make their home here and many tiny side trails lead down to the water's edge, a haven for fishing enthusiasts.

A frisky squirrel scampered across our path and up a tree, proudly displaying a large nut in his mouth.

This trail is absolutely one of the best beginner trails that we have explored, a great nature lesson for children, and a chance, in this instance, to point out the dangers of swift water.

All along the trail were early wildflowers. There were groups of Bloodroot – a white fragile flower that closes at night, that is about one and one half inches wide, and blooms from March to May. The juice of the underground stem is red and notably used by Indians for dying baskets, clothing, and for use as war paint and insect repellent.

There were yellow Trout Lilies and Cowslips, pretty pink Round-lobed Hepaticas and purple Violets.

At a lookout area, we met a friendly birdwatcher peering through his binoculars. He told us where we could find the best patch of Trilliums, some red ones, but to our disappointment when we got there, the buds had not opened.

Although we didn't see any beaver in the area, small tree trunks had been chomped almost to a point at the centre by sharp teeth, leaving the tree unable to sustain its upright position and causing it to fall over.

Farther along the trail is part of an old concrete dam that juts midway into the creek. Here you can walk along its base, or walk along the narrow top (not recommended).

Soon you will come to Cleaver Road and a bridge. Make a left and again pick up the trail leading back to the Nature Center. This southern side of the creek is a little more rugged as you pass through a white pine forest with a carpet of pine needles, and a trail that is not as commonly used.

Although, there are some side trails leading out to the water's edge, these are not part of the main trail. It is possible to get a little confused as there are no signs, but it is safe enough if you pick the trail that appears to have had the most traffic.

Here, in a small clearing, we spotted a hut that had been constructed out of fallen tree branches and twigs. As we approached the fire pit you could imagine the smell of fresh fish cooking over an open flame. I called out as we approached, "Anyone home?" But it appeared that the sometime-residents had been washed out with mud from the spring rains.

It's about here where you will see Private Property signs posted on trees. Stick to the main trail and climb up to the ridge that looks down on the creek below. On this last leg of our hike we could hear in the distance the frog serenade telling us that we were nearing the Mill site.

Back again at the bridge, we decided to retrace our steps to the Mill and have lunch there, rather than eat at the public picnic area near the Nature Center.

We found the Mill setting so peaceful and with a couple of benches and a close-up view to study the old Mill construction, it beat television any day.

Stopping to explore, take photos and eat lunch, this trail took us two and a half hours of pleasant fresh air and exercise.

DeCew Falls

7.
DeCew Falls on the Bruce Trail

Difficulty: Beginner. The hike into the falls on the Bruce Trail and back to DeCew Road should only take about two hours of easy walking.
Directions: Take the QEW to Exit 49 and travel through St. Catharines on Hwy. 406. Exit at St. David's Rd. and turn right. Drive a short way to Merrittville Hwy. and turn left. When you arrive at DeCew Rd., turn right. Watch for the river and parking lot on your right. Here is where you pick up the link to the Bruce Trail, north. No admission fees.

It was overcast and there was a raw wind blowing out of the east as we once again hauled out our winter coats and gloves.

April had tricked us a couple of days before into thinking summer was here, or at the very least, spring had arrived. Determined to go on a hike, we grabbed our gear and headed for St. Catharines.

Not for a minute did we suspect that we were running headlong into what turned out to be one of our most risky experiences. Hiking is not a walk in the park. Risks are what make hiking so appealing, but being prepared for those risks is what keeps you out of trouble. I don't know how many times I have thanked our boots for getting us out of a sticky situation.

The link to the Bruce Trail that takes you into DeCew Falls and the flour mill is located on DeCew

Road about 45 minutes from the Burlington Skyway Bridge. There are two trails. Take the trail that runs along the west side of the river that links Lake Moodie and Lake Gibson.

There is a parking area on your right, alongside the stone ruins of the DeCew family home, destroyed by fire about 50 years ago. There are no washrooms or maps. Just follow the trail that heads north along the shores of the river. Check the trees for the white rectangle of paint, familiar signs of the Bruce Trail.

Soon, you will come to a left turn over a gravelled dam, constructed for Ontario Hydro and you will see their large brick facilities as you walk along the dam.

Go as far as you can: You'll see a path leading down off the dam to your left and into the woods.

The trail is easy walking with hard packed-earth and tree roots, and fairly flat. About an hour into your hike you'll come to a T in the trail. Turn left and you'll begin to hear the rumble of the lower falls. It is barely visible through the trees atop a 66-foot ravine.

Follow the trail and in a few minutes you will arrive at the DeCew Falls and the Mill site. A more picturesque setting you will never see. We were there before the leaves on the trees had fully opened, so it may be difficult to see it during the summer months.

I took some photos, then wandered around the buildings, searching in vain for a way down to the bottom of the falls for a closer look. There are plans to build a circular staircase down the 66-foot drop, replacing stairs that had been there many years ago. Unfortunately, there were no signs of construction. We had made up our minds that the one-hour trek was well worth the trip, so we happily started retracing our steps for the one-hour trek back to our vehicle.

Photography being one of my reasons for hiking, I kept my eyes peeled looking down to the base of the gorge for a path that might lead us down to the lower falls. Leaving the upper falls behind, we spotted a trail that promised to lead us down to the base of the gorge. It looked to be harmless enough.

Hard-packed earth and tree roots to act as steps down a very steep incline couldn't be all that bad. In my eagerness to get that perfect photograph, I sometimes forget the dangers and my fear of heights.

At one point I was poised, camera to my face, and leaning against a tree that was at a 45-degree angle over the edge of the ridge, with my husband hanging on to the hood of my jacket. Descending into the gorge, we picked our way down to a flat area, but the 40 remaining feet was over loose shale rock, wet leaves, tree roots and mud.

Finally, we arrived at the creek bed and, concentrating on every step, we slipped and stumbled over rock and fallen logs, back toward the lower falls.

My excitement grew with the roar of the falls as it appeared through the trees and then, suddenly, a 15-foot wide mudslide from the top of the ridge blocked our path. With no way around, or over it, and perhaps risking our life and limb even to get to this point, we had no choice but to turn back.

It crossed my mind then that if an injury had occurred, we were in a very isolated area with no chance of anyone hearing our whistle over the roar of the raging water. We found the spot where we had descended, looked up at the steep wall of the gorge, took a deep breath and climbed to the top. I turned and looked down to where we had been. I could not believe that we had accomplished that trek without a scratch, thanks to our boots, cardio endurance and some good leg muscles. What a trip!

The hike, including our trek to the bottom of the gorge, took us three hours.

Take my advice: Wait until they construct that circular staircase, and stick to the main trail.

Woodend Conservation Area

8.
Woodend Conservation Area Bruce Trail Link

Difficulty: Intermediate/Beginner
Directions: Take QEW Niagara and exit at Glendale Ave. Travel west a short distance to a traffic light intersection with Niagara College Campus on your left. Turn left here on Beechwood Ave. (not marked when we were there) and head south. As you go up the hill, watch for the green sign Woodend Conservation on your left. Turn in and park on the side of the road, before you get to the steel gate entrance. You pick up the Bruce Trail, left of the gate. No admission fee.

The Woodend Conservation near St. Catharines, about 45 minutes from the Burlington Skyway Bridge, has a number of trails that are not clearly marked.

All of the short beginner trails eventually lead back to the Homestead, or the parking areas, so you really can't get lost, but some of the plastic colour coded arrows that indicates a specific trail have been ripped away, leaving room for confusion if you are a first time visitor.

We thoroughly scouted the six miles of trails in order to give you some consistency to what you will find there and the trail that I would recommend for its points of interest and a spectacular variety of spring wild flowers is the Bruce Trail. It borders the entire

Woodend Conservation Area and follows the edge of the escarpment, letting you to see the points of interest that Woodend offers. The trail surface consists of hard packed-earth, tree roots and rocks. The Bruce Trail begins just as you pull off Beechwood Road, at the steel gate entrance to the conservation area.

Look to your left of the gate and you will see a trail with the familiar white painted rectangles of the Bruce Trail painted on trees. These markings are the only ones here that are clear and easy to follow.

As you meander along the trail, masses of wild flowers are everywhere. We were there the end of April and even then, many of the flowers were in bloom, with hundreds more to follow in coming weeks.

As you look down the trail, you will come to a Y, take the trail to the left and keep to the left along the escarpment edge. Here you will see spectacular rock formations, which have slipped away from their home as part of the escarpment, creating gigantic crevices and huge overhangs of layered rock, seemingly, suspended in mid air. Warning signs along the way indicate that those ledges may be unstable, as weathering and erosion is taking its toll. Coral fossils suggest this area was covered by a shallow tropical sea 450 million years ago.

About 45 minutes into your hike, look down to your left, and watch for the ruins of a limestone kiln, just below the escarpment edge. To the right of the trail in this general location stands the Interpretive Center built on lands settled by the United Empire Loyalists in the late 1700's. In 1796, the Van Every family was granted the land. The existing buildings were established by their descendents, the Thomsons, in 1932. The Conservation Authority then purchased the property in 1974. The large white building is truly impressive, surrounded by remains of old stonewalls and perennial gardens. There is also a pet cemetery.

You have hiked now for about an hour and a stop for lunch on a bench there might be just the breather you may need, as the remainder of the loop is a little more rugged, with some incline towards the end. After you leave the bench, still following the Bruce Trail, you will veer to your left and start descending down into the valley. It's sad to look up and see the erosion chipping away the face of the escarpment and you may wonder how long it will remain a hiker's paradise.

Wild flowers are in abundance here, as well, with Jack-in-the-pulpit being one I hadn't seen for some time. Trilliums were just beginning to burst open, with other varieties still in bud. Farther along this same stretch there will be another trail to the left, leading farther down into the valley. That trail is not part of the loop that returns you to the parking area where you came in.

There is a short stretch of incline walking near the end of your hike, to deliver you back to the top of the escarpment and the road. When you reach the road, turn left to head back to the steel gate entrance where you began the Bruce Trail and parked your vehicle.

The entire loop of the Bruce Trail will take approximately two hours of hiking, taking time to explore, eat lunch and take photographs. If you find that you are tired at the Homestead location, which is about the halfway mark of the loop, walk through the parking lot there and follow the road back to the steel gate entrance and your vehicle. and the only outhouse-type washrooms were located at the Information and Interpretive centre.

Children of all ages must be closely supervised at all times, on all hikes, and pets must be on a leash. There are no fences or guard rails along the edge of the escarpment. It sometimes can be rugged and dangerous.

Sherman Falls

9.
Tiffany Falls Trail
and Sherman Falls Trail

Difficulty: Advanced. The round trip into both falls took us two and half hours.

Directions: Take Main St. W. in Hamilton. Follow it until it turns into Wilson St. towards Ancaster. Head up the escarpment and on the right you will pass a greenhouse and nursery. Just a short distance beyond, watch for the pull-off area for Tiffany Falls on your left. (Shown in photo at left: Sherman Falls)
Or, from Hwy 403, take Mohawk Rd. W., the name changes to Rousseaux St. in Ancaster. Follow it until you come to Wilson St., turn right, and head down the escarpment. Watch for the Tiffany Falls sign and the pull-off area on your right. Both falls can be accessed from this parking lot. There is no admission fee.

May 1st is locked away in our memories book as one of the most rewarding and spectacular days since we started hiking three years ago. We have driven through Ancaster many times, unaware of two waterfalls that will actually trap you in the moment and make you reluctant to leave them behind.

Tiffany Falls is in the Tiffany Conservation Area just off Wilson St. in Ancaster. It has a total height of approximately 24.5 metres (80.3 ft) and the best times to view are spring and fall.

We began our hike at a pull-off area on Wilson where there is an information sign for Tiffany Falls.

The Tiffany Falls trail starts off with hard-packed earth, tree roots and rocks, with a gentle roll to the up and down hill grades. Soon you will come to an area where the trail has been washed away due to erosion and from here you need to be an experienced hiker with good hiking boots. The sign indicated that due to the loss of the path, the trail crossed the creek in two places. But on descending to the creek bed, how and where you crossed the creek was left up to you.

The fast-flowing creek had slick rocks and deep holes, so picking where to cross was a lesson on safety. Fallen trees were a challenge, and the muddy riverbank was slippery with wet leaves and hidden rocks. Our boots again saved us from injury and wet feet.

Soon, we caught up with two ladies sitting on a large flat rock at the base of the falls, and we all agreed it was well worth the hike. They asked us questions about other trails in the area and told us that they were tourists from Australia taking a six-week vacation in Ontario. I asked them how this trail compared to trails in Australia. They looked around at the terrain they gave a resounding, "Some are worse."

"We generally hike with hiking gloves to protect our hands from having to grasp rocks and trees to aid us in some inclines," one lady said. "But today we didn't think we'd need them and left them in the car."

I reached for my camera, hoping photos would act as reminders of the fresh smell of tumbling water and cool, gentle spray hitting my face. The trail back was no less difficult. The round trip took about an hour.

Directly north, across Wilson St. from the pull-off area at Tiffany Falls, there is a sign for the Bruce Trail (Sherman Falls), which leads down wooden steps into the forest. This trail, again, should be traveled by experienced hikers and consists of hard-packed earth, tree roots, rocks and climbing. As you trek along the path you can look down into the valley below, or up and see the guardrails along Wilson St.

About 20 minutes into the hike, you will cross a small stream that is flowing down into the valley from a culvert under the highway. No spring flowers were in bloom. But an array of shrubs with sharp thorns; berry bushes and young trees lined this old nature trail. But a couple of old discarded tires and an old rusty safe reminded us we were still in the modern world.

We soon crossed Old Dundas Rd. and picked up the Bruce Trail that follows Ancaster Creek into Sherman Falls. We had only walked a few feet when through the leafless trees I yelled "There it is!"

Sherman Falls, not to be outdone by Tiffany Falls, was another breathtaking view. Here the trail is easier to navigate and there's a bridge where you can stand to take photos of the falls, or cross the creek to rejoin a continuation of the Bruce Trail.

If you choose to continue, the Bruce Trail will lead you up a steep grade, makes a sharp right and passes along private property. Here we stopped and returned to the falls. If you look up to your right, you will see a lookout area, which I believe is located on private property and not accessible. We sat just beyond the bridge and ate our lunch, all the while in silence, overwhelmed by the thundering sound and the unforgettable view of the cascading falls.

The hike to Sherman Falls from the Tiffany Falls pull-off area is approximately 40 minutes. Peering over our shoulders, reluctant to leave, we began the hike back to our vehicle. Along the way we tracked deer hoof prints in the mud on numerous spots along the path.

Both trails are for experienced hikers. It's advisable to know your abilities and never hike alone.

Crawford Lake

10.
Crawford Lake Trails

Difficulty: Beginner/Intermediate/Advanced
Directions: From the QEW. take Guelph Line North at Burlington (Exit 102). You will cross over Hwy. #5. From this point you will travel 14 km north to Steeles Ave. Turn right (east) at the Crawford Lake Conservation sign on Steeles Ave., and continue to the park entrance. Admission charges apply.

Sometimes, without planning it, a hike turns out to be a perfect day full of extraordinary beauty, educational adventure, and a cardio workout geared to your fitness level. The third week in May gave us a sunny, cool, spring morning and a day to remember.

Crawford Lake near Milton has it all, plus it has one of the most documented and perfectly marked trail systems, we have yet discovered. There are five colour coded trails at Crawford Lake, all perfectly marked and branching out from the Visitor Centre, which holds a gift shop, washroom facilities, telephone and maps.

The Crawford Lake Trail colour coded in blue, is an elevated boardwalk that surrounds the entire lake, is wheelchair accessible and great for children of all ages. The boardwalk was constructed to preserve the delicate shoreline, and lush forest. There are several seating areas along the walk, which provides a scenic rest area, with information boards explaining the formation of the lake and the human history.

Crawford Lake is 24 metres (79 feet) deep and rare in that, it contains environmental information dating as far back as 1,000 years. Because there is very little circulation and limited oxygen below 15 metres (49 feet), nothing grows or survives in the oxygen-poor water, so all of the annual deposits of sediment are similar to growth rings on a tree, allowing accurate dating of the layered bands. The lake floor is a time capsule and through studies of the sediment it allowed researchers to discover the Iroquoian village, which has been reconstructed near the Visitor Centre.

It was an enjoyable 45-minute walk. Unusual tree and rock formations added interest to the awakening landscape. Jewelled water glistened in spring sunlight.

If the fresh air has spurred you on for another trail, the Woodland Trail, colour coded in red is a 45-minute loop on hard-packed earth. It's also wheelchair accessible, with scenic woods and wetlands.

Still another trail, Pine Ridge Trail, colour coded in green, is about a one hour and 30 minute loop, which provides a hike through rolling woodlands, a pine forest, open fields and out to a glacial ridge with a wonderful view of the escarpment. This trail begins and ends on the Woodland Trail.

The Escarpment Trail, colour coded in yellow is about a one hour hike, more rugged and rocky as it winds its way along the edge of the escarpment, where information cairns and benches are located. All of these trails loop back to the Visitor Centre.

After we left Crawford Lake Trail, we took the Nassagaweya Trail, colour coded in orange. This is a two-to three-hour hike one-way to Rattlesnake Point. This trail does not loop. You must return the same way The round trip can take 4-6 hours. We did it in four.

The trail starts off easy walking and you begin to think it's a piece of cake, but don't be fooled. This trail crosses the Nassagaweya Canyon and has everything an experienced hiker could wish for.

At times, the trail ahead looked more like a rock pile, but slowly we could make out areas where we could place our feet and pick our way down to the floor of the canyon. Rocks and tree roots gave us the footholds we needed to climb. The landscape, with its gorgeous variety of wildflowers, was astonishing.

I had never seen pink trilliums, and, as we approached a boardwalk, it looked like someone's perfectly landscaped backyard, all done by the miracle of nature with yellow Marsh Marigolds.

As we started the climb up to Rattlesnake Point, we spotted a clearing at the edge of the escarpment, and, to get a closer look at the valley we had just climbed out of, we went to the edge to investigate.

Suddenly, too close for comfort, a huge bird took flight just as we approached. A Turkey Vulture with a wingspan of about six feet glided silently over our heads and swooped down into a tree to join three others, perched high among the branches. Their claws looked big enough to carry a human. After our shock of seeing that gigantic bird so close, I realized I'd missed the perfect photo, forgetting my camera was dangling from my shoulder in the locked position, I complained about my stupidity throughout the hike.

Soon we reached a lookout with a panoramic view and large rocks for sitting, but since we had not reached our destination, we decided to move on with a promise to return there for lunch.

Another 20 minutes took us to Rattlesnake Point, a terrific view, and much needed washrooms. We returned to that picturesque lookout, enjoyed our lunch and rested before the long hike back.

The return trip was no less challenging and I again searched for those Turkey Vultures, but they were long gone.

I highly recommend all of these trails, but always consider the time involved and your fitness level. It is very easy to overtax yourself. Time goes by quickly when you are hiking – and you must leave enough energy for the return trip.

11.
Red Hill Valley Trail

Difficulty: Beginner/Intermediate (flat surfaces with steep inclines)
Directions: Highway 403, then Lincoln Alexander Expressway towards Hamilton. Exit at Dartnall Rd., left on Stone Church, and left on Pritchard Rd. Make a right onto Mud St. and the Red Hill Valley Trail parking lot is on your left. To reach Albion Falls and Buttermilk Falls, turn right out of the parking lot and follow Mud St. until it turns into Mountain Brow Blvd. Both parking lots are on your right. No admission fee.

    Like some of you, we arrive at trail locations unfamiliar with the area and hoping for a rewarding day of exploration, exercise and fresh air. But at times, frustration is added to the experience.
    Mid-May presented one of those days. The day began well, turning warm and sunny after a week of cold and rain. Like most hiking locations, we found trails in every direction. But they weren't properly marked and it quickly became a guessing game.
    We arrived at the Red Hill Valley parking lot on Mud St. around 9:30 a.m. Early mornings are the best times to hike: If you lose your way or take the wrong route, daylight can assist your return to your vehicle.
    As we started our hike, we realized two points of interest – Albion Falls and Buttermilk Falls – weren't

accessible from the Red Hill Valley Trail parking lot. We turned right back onto Mud St. and drove west a short distance, rounded a bend onto Mountain Brow Blvd., and crossed over a cement bridge.

On the right, we could see a gorge below. We turned into Kings Forest parking lot just beyond and found a spectacular view of Albion Falls.

But to get a closer look, we walked back along the bridge to a set of steel steps leading part way down to the base of the falls.

As we exited the steel steps, we spotted a parking lot directly across the road. There were no signs so we assumed it was the entrance to Buttermilk Falls. We hiked over a bridge, which crossed Red Hill Creek, and did a long incline walk only to find ourselves in a residential area, with no falls.

Retracing our steps, we walked along Mountain Brow Blvd., past the lot where we'd parked. We then discovered Buttermilk Falls only 10 minutes away.

Buttermilk is a small ribbon falls, fed by a tributary of Red Hill Creek. It must have been gigantic at one time by the look of the deep, bowl-shaped gorge. I expected a larger falls and was disappointed to see grotesque graffiti painted just at the point where the water emerged from beneath the bridge.

As we arrived back at our vehicle we noticed a trail leading off along the escarpment. It was clearly marked with blue rectangles, a sign of a link to the Bruce Trail. We hoped it might lead back to the Mud St. parking lot where the Red Hill Valley Trail begins.

After 30 minutes, we found this trail was leading us in the wrong direction. We returned to our vehicle, drove back to the lot on Mud St., and began our hike.

The Red Hill Valley Trail base is easy walking, consisting of tar and gravel. It's also very clean, thanks to the Friends of the Red Hill Valley (volunteers) who happened to be there that day, gathering up garbage.

After crossing an open field, we descended a steep slope into the valley. A short way down, you'll see a trail leading off to the right without signs or trail indicators. Stick to what appears to be the main trail.

At the base is a T-intersection at the edge of a golf course, again, no trail indicators, so we made a guess and turned right. Flat easy walking was on the menu for about 40 minutes until we came to a fork in the trail, one prong leading over a bridge and the other continuing straight. "Go straight," a fellow hiker told us, and that will take you to an underpass at King St.

But after 20 minutes of uphill climbing we knew we had been given the wrong information: We were in another residential area. Retracing our steps, we found the trail over the bridge was the way to King St.

Tired now, and frustrated by the lack of trail markers, we stopped at the creek, ate lunch and began our return hike. Although bewildered newcomers to this trail, our hike was made more enjoyable by wild flowers, a squirrel, two mallard ducks, a woodpecker, two falcons, and a couple of friendly hikers.

When you get back to the golf course and the T-intersection where you originally came down, go straight and follow another trail which is more visually interesting, or take the same trail. They both will take you back to Mud St. and the parking lot. Because you descended into the valley you will be doing a steady uphill climb and going up is a lot harder than going down. The climb would be difficult for small children.

The Red Hill Valley Trail is about 7 km. or 4.3 miles. We had intended to hike the entire length of the trail. But having to retrace our footsteps turned a two-hour hike into four. This is what can happen if you are new to the area, and there are no trail markers. So, be prepared to spend more time than you had planned for. Also, make it a practice to tell someone about the area in which you're hiking, in case you're late returning.

12.
Dundas Valley
Headwaters Trail:

Difficulty: Advanced
Directions: From Hwy. 403 take Hwy. 52 to Copetown, turn right on Governors Rd. (Regional Rd. 299) to the main entrance of the Conservation area. There's an admission fee at the automated gate entry.

    A day ending the month of May started out sunny, with a stunning blue-sky and a moderate cool breeze blowing out of the north. We had done the Main Loop, and the Spring Creek Trail weeks before, but today we decided to explore the Headwaters Trail, another one of many trails in the area.

    Dundas Valley has approximately 40 km (24.9 miles) of trails dispersed over 1,012 hectares (2,500 acres), so picking a trail geared to your endurance level is your top priority. The problem is, until you have done the trail, or someone has described it to you, you are at the mercy of knowledge provided by maps, which you can pick up at the Visitor Centre, a reproduction of a Victorian railway station.

    According to the basic map we had, the Headwaters Trail branched off from the Main Loop Trail just before arriving at a parking lot. We trudged off happily, thinking the information we had could not be wrong. From the Visitor Center, we crossed over the Hamilton Brantford Rail Trail, walking in a southeasterly direction, and picked up the Main Loop Trail, which according to our map would lead us to the beginning of the Headwaters Trail. In about 20 minutes we arrived at a parking lot, noticed that a trail marker had been taken off a post and presumed it to be the Headwaters Trail indicator. The map showed that the trail crossed over two paved roads, so we went through the parking area and looked beyond to find another trail marker. Thinking we'd somehow missed it we turned right out of the parking lot and walked along the edge of the road hoping to pick up the trail.

In about an hour we found ourselves back at the Visitor Center, frustrated beyond belief. We again examined the large map posted outside the Center and still confused, I stomped into the building, hoping the kind person at the desk could figure out what we had done wrong. It became clear then, that there were two parking lots, the one we were at was not shown on the map and that we had not gone far enough along the Main Loop Trail.

We discovered that the Head Waters Trail was a 10 km (6.25 mile) hike and we had already wasted an hour of our predicted hiking time. It was 11:30 a.m., a bit late to start on such a long trail with no idea of the terrain. It was risky, but we decided it was probably an easy hike, and that we should return in late afternoon.

There were more runners and cyclists in the area than usual: There was an endurance event going on that sent exercise enthusiasts over 100 miles (160 km) of trail and far into the night. We did not know that our endurance would be tested many times over.

We stayed on the Main Loop, past the parking lot where we had made our mistake, crossed over a bridge at a small stream, climbed a steep winding hill and soon arrived at the entrance to the Headwaters Trail. It looked harmless enough. Good trail surface with hard packed earth, a few small rocks and tree roots, nothing very scenic, just a walk in the woods.

Runners were passing by with a friendly wave or hello, even the cyclists managed to acknowledge us as they sped by. About an hour into the trail we came across one of the stations set up for food, drink, and first aid for the participants of the race.

At this point there was a crossing of trails with no trail indicators, so we asked which one was the Headwaters Trail. They got out their map, pointed straight ahead and got us on our way, but their map indicated there was a large loop at the end of the trail where all of the race enthusiasts were heading. What the heck, if these people were running it, surely we could walk it. We were amazed at the physical ability of some of the runners, many gray-haired, and aging, with most of the younger adults riding trail bikes.Headwaters Trail is a continuous hill and valley uphill climb to the very top of the escarpment, and then around a large loop, which took us about two hours, eventually returning us to the link leading us back to the Main Loop Trail and the Visitor Center. The Headwaters Trail is one of the most physically challenging trails we have found. I confess that as I sit and write this today, my muscles are telling me that we made it, but not by much.

We hiked it in four hours and returned to our vehicle, feeling our legs were just instruments holding us up. Tired, and cold from a wind blowing out of the north, we still couldn't believe our good luck. Just at the very moment I closed the truck door and we were in the safety and comfort of our vehicle, came the rain.

If you're looking for a trail to test your physical endurance level, this is the trail. Remember, check the time you begin, and save energy for the return trip. Turn back if you think you've overextended yourself.

The Hermitage

13.
Dundas Valley
Main Loop Trail:

Difficulty: Beginner to intermediate
Directions: From 403, take Hwy. 52 to Copetown, turn right on Governors Rd. (Regional Rd. 299) to the main entrance of the Conservation area. There is an admission fee.

The Dundas Valley Trails consist of a maze of seven trails, including the Main Loop Trail, an introductory trail, which we decided to explore in May.

There's also the Spring Creek Trail, Monarch Trail, Heritage Trail, Headwaters Trail, McCormack Trail, and the Hamilton Brantford Rail Trail.

The picturesque Visitor Center (an interesting reproduction of a Victorian railway station) provides washrooms, picnic tables, light lunches, and free maps. Before starting the hike, I strongly suggest that you obtain a map of the area.

Stay on the trails, and pay close attention to the symbols marking the trail that you have chosen. It could be a brightly colored circle or stripes of paint on a tree. Taking pictures, or finding interesting foliage or flowers can take your attention away from where you are walking, so when you come to a fork in the road do not quickly assume that you have made the right choice of path. Take a look at your map, and check the trail symbol. At this point, as at the start of the trail, check your watch for the correct time.

The Main Loop Trail is well traveled and marked with a red circle on a square sign, mounted on a post. The path is constructed of hard-packed gravel, and is easy walking. Periodically you'll come to another trail that branches off, and they're usually clearly marked.

We also came across other hikers, cyclists, and horseback riders, and we walked through the stone ruins of the Hermitage, an 1855 summer estate of the Leith family, long ago destroyed by fire.

Wild purple violets lined the path, forget-me-nots formed soft blue clouds on the forest floor, and wild geraniums were everywhere. A couple of steep grades got our hearts pumping, and a drink of water, from our generous supply, was a welcome treat.

About an hour into our hike we came to a fork in the trail, quickly glanced at the post with the red circle, and confidently took the path to the right. The scenery and trail almost immediately, became more rugged. We began a steady upward climb, which we assumed was the intermediate part of the trail. Rocks as big as houses, covered in green moss had broken away from the main part of the escarpment, leaving deep caverns and interesting formations.

Spread out below us on the valley floor was an enchanted forest of green shapes and textures. It was unnaturally quiet. We found the perfect place to perch on a fallen log and eat a lunch of egg salad sandwiches and whole strawberries. Returning two of the largest strawberries to our lunch bag, I jokingly announced that, if we got lost, we'd have food for dinner.

Soon I realized we had not seen a red circle for a long time. The only markings were white painted rectangles, we knew as being indicators of the Bruce

Trail, which bordered other trails in the area, so we continued for about an hour, all the while looking for a link to get us back to the information centre.

Checking our map, we discovered we had been walking in the wrong direction, and would have to retrace our route back to where we had made our mistake. Those two strawberries were beginning to look more and more like the main meal of the day. We were a little worried now. Since we had not checked the time at the fork in the trail, we headed back.

Even experienced hikers can get into trouble, so plan your hike, take plenty of food and water and make sure you follow the trail you have chosen.

Yes, hiking is truly an adventure of unexpected proportions.

Exactly four hours of beginner, intermediate, and advanced climbing later, we were again back at the beginning of the Main Loop Trail, and saw a young deer watching us from the edge of an apple orchard. At this point does the old saying, "Do as I say, not as I do," ring a bell?

The Main Loop Trail, 3.5 km., would have only taken us, at a moderate walk, about an hour and a half.

14.
Valens Conservation Boardwalk Trail:

Difficulty: Beginner, ideal for all family members.
Directions: From Hwy. 403, take Hwy. 6 north, turn left on Regional Rd. 97 and follow signs. Admission charges apply.

Could it be that summer had finally arrived the first week in June, after we had been tricked numerous times with cool temperatures and windy conditions?

To better take advantage of the remarkable sunny skies and warm breezes, we collected our hiking gear and made straight for the Valens Conservation Area, just east of Cambridge. This was to be our first visit, and what a surprise. The Boardwalk Trail and the log cabin are indeed two of the area's many highlights.

As you pass by the ticket booth, look to your right and on a hill nestled into a grove of trees you will see a historical log cabin, built by Mr. George Cook Senior. He was born in Ireland in 1791, immigrated to Canada with his family around 1842, but sadly, his wife died at sea during the trip. He settled in Beverly Township with his children, and then around 1848 he married Martha Taylor, a resident of West Flamborough.

His cabin was moved to the site by Conservation Authorities, and is an accurate depiction of a home during the 1842 to 1885 period. The contents, donated by several different donors, give an overall view of furnishings from the mid 1800's to the early 1900's.

Continuing along the roadway you will pass the parking area for the beach, but turn into the next parking lot for boat rentals and look for four large rocks at the far end of the parking lot. This is the beginning of the Boardwalk Trail.

Within a few feet along this path emerges a spectacular walking bridge that expands the entire width of the lake. Looking down into the clear shallow waters we could see fish approximately 18 inches (45 cm) long, swimming in pairs and we could hear the frenzied splash of their spawning rituals in the tall weeds along the shore. Fishing at the time was prohibited between May 1st and June 30th for this spawning ritual to occur.

After leaving the bridge, turn to your left and follow along the shores of the lake. There we came upon a group of children receiving canoeing lessons, under the watchful eye of conservation experts. Soon, the trail passes by a stone ruin that had probably been a foundation for a barn, or house, which had sadly, crumbled under the stress of time.

Keep in mind, if there is a branching off of another trail that is not posted as the Boardwalk Trail, choose the one that is closest to the lake. It is easy walking, through grass, hard packed earth, tree roots, and a pine needle carpet. Red Trilliums had been in full bloom a few weeks before, but now looked faded and dreary. There are many benches along this trail, to allow you to rest, or take in the view.

Father along, you will come to a 300-metre (984-foot) boardwalk, an ideal spot to sit patiently waiting for birds and wildlife to make an appearance, and although there are no railings along this boardwalk, it is of sturdy construction and provides plenty of room for two people to pass. For the first time this year, we had our first encounter with mosquitoes, located mainly in the shaded, cool areas of the trail, so don't forget to pack the bug repellent.

Through about a third of the hike, there is a branching off to the left of the main path. That short trail leads you out to a lookout tower that provides a full view of the lake. The day we were there a guided tour was underway, taking a group of children on a nature hike. After leaving the lookout tower, proceed along the trail next to the lake, and off in the distance you will see the familiar sight of the bridge you crossed at the beginning of the hike.

At the end of the trail we walked along a grass path, across an open area and spotted a brilliant yellow Goldfinch, calmly sitting on a low branch of a small shrub. We stopped and watched him, marvelling at his spectacular colour. Here, at the bridge you will return to the parking lot and your vehicle. The complete trip around the lake took us one hour and 20 minutes. Other highlights in the area can turn your hike into a full day of boating, picnicking, and swimming.

The beach is safe and sandy and has a special screen that separates the swimming area from the rest of the lake. This allows the water for the swimming area to be chlorinated. Camping is also permitted in the specified campgrounds, maintaining the overall clean and well-kept appearance of this magnificent outdoor experience. Washrooms are dispersed throughout the park. There are also other trails in the area with information and maps available at the entrance to the Conservation Area.

Canoes, rowboats, and paddleboats, are available for rental. In winter, you can snowshoe, ski, or winter hike, or relax by the wood stove with hot chocolate at the pavilion. Valens Conservation Area is open year-round from 8 am to sunset, except for Christmas Day.

15
Westfield Woods Trail:

Difficulty: Beginner
Directions: From Hwy. 403 take Hwy. 6 north. Turn left (west) on Hwy. 5 and then right (north) on Hwy 8. Turn right on Concession #6. There are no trail signs, just watch for a parking area on your right.

From the corner of Hwy. 5 and Hwy. 6 to the trail entrance, travel time is about 30 minutes. The Westfield Heritage Village is completely operational on Sundays and holidays from March to October between 12:30 and 4 p.m. All other days, buildings are closed, but you can walk through the village depositing an honorary fee. On Sundays and holidays an admission fee applies at the entrance.

It had rained heavily the night before and a soft mist and fog still lingered in an early morning the first week in June.

Hiking in bad weather is not always unpleasant. It can add a haunting cast to photographs and tweak a new sense of adventure.

As with every trail, an element of unpredictability is always present, so be prepared for any situation even if you think you will only be out a short time.

Maps can be wrong and getting disoriented in a maze of unmarked trails can be unnerving and take away your enjoyment of the hike. To avoid getting hurt or lost, never start a hike without water, food, compass, first-aid kit, bug repellent, and rain gear.

Before we left that morning, we checked the map we had of the Westfield Woods Trail near Rockton, a beginner trail about 5 km (3.1 miles) long.

Since I'd caught a flu bug two weeks before, I wasn't feeling confident about my energy level, so we picked this trail as something of an easy trek. How wrong we were.

The beginning of the trail starts off on Concession #6 just east of Hwy #8. There are no signs, but keep looking to your right and in about five minutes you will see a parking area large enough for three or four vehicles with a chain barricade across the path.

The trail leads through the woods in a southerly direction (check your compass) so to return go in the opposite direction, which in this case would be north.

By now the clouds had parted allowing sunlight to streak through the trees, promising better weather for our hike. We walked for about 20 minutes on hard-packed gravel and noticed a small sign that read "to Village" pointing to the left. We knew that Westfield Heritage Village was near the trail, so we decided to check it out and then return to our original hike.

The village was absolutely the highlight of our day. The heritage buildings in the village are only open on Sundays and holidays, but you can walk through the village anytime on any other day, leaving an honorary fee. The sugar shack, train station, log chapel and schoolhouse were my favourites. The streets harkened back to a time when things were less complicated, I had an overwhelming urge to stay.

Soon, we retraced our steps back to the Westfield Woods Trail and turning left we again began our hike.

All along this path, in large groups, were wild rose bushes loaded with buds and as we passed, the sweet smell of rose drifted in the air. One flower had opened, giving us a promise of what was yet to come in the following weeks, when all the other buds would burst forth with the overpowering, delightful smell.

In about 30 minutes, we came to a gigantic oak tree and barn ruins with two trails, one leading to the left and one off to the right, providing no indication of where either would lead us. Because the trail to the left had been most traveled we took that one, hoping it was the main loop trail. Here there was an abundance of lilac bushes with spent blooms and we imagined how spectacular the sight and smell would have been a couple of weeks earlier.

Soon the trail became muddy and took us farther into a swampy area swarming with a large population of mosquitoes.

After 40 minutes, we came to a paved highway and with a sinking feeling, retraced our steps back to the oak tree and the barn ruins.

Again we checked our map and took the trail to the right of the ruins, expecting that it could only be the one that made up the main loop trail.

The farther we went, the denser the underbrush became. Worse, in trying to find the trail through the high grass after the rain, our pant legs were soaked. We knew we were still on some sort of trail, but there were areas where we had to duck under shrubs and trip through tangled weeds.

Suddenly we entered a clearing. Adding confusion to insult, we discovered two more unmarked trails. We desperately checked the compass for the umpteenth time. We knew we had to return north and kept to the trail heading in that direction.

To our dismay we arrived at a farmer's cornfield. More than two hours had passed. I was exhausted from my bout with the flu. This trail didn't seem to be leading us anywhere.

Again we retraced our steps, checked the compass and although we were disoriented, we weren't entirely lost as we could hear the traffic on Highway #8. If we became desperate we could go there, find Concession #6 and return to our vehicle. But still, Hwy. 8, was a long way off.

Determined to find the main loop, we finally came to a clearing and I noticed hydro poles and wires, which could only mean we were coming to a road.

Sure enough, another 20 minutes brought us out onto Concession #6 about a mile west of where our vehicle was parked.

We never did find the main loop trail. I was completely exhausted by the time we got to our truck. I realized more fully what it means to never know what to expect on a hike. It should have only taken an hour, but instead took us three.

This trail is easy walking to the village and onward toward the oak tree and the barn ruins.

But from there, go back the same way you came. The rest of the trail – certainly the part we walked – is a nightmare.

16
Crook's Hollow Historical Trail:

Difficulty: Beginner
Directions: Hwy. 401 take Hwy 6 South, turn right on Hwy 5, and then left on Brock Rd. and right on Old Brock Rd. Old Brock Rd. curves to the right but drive straight through the intersection, to arrive at the parking lot on your left. Admission is voluntary.

It was an unusually cool day for the first week in July, as we arrived at the parking lot just outside the village of Greensville.

Hiking in the morning is our best time. It is cool, trails are not crowded, and it is the best time to shoot photos, while taking advantage of the yellow light of the morning sun.

Crook's Hollow Historical Trail links the Bruce Trail, Christie Conservation Area, Spencer Gorge, Tews and Webster's Falls, and the historic village of Greensville, Ontario, located on Highway #8.

It is curious to note that the quiet Crooks' Hollow was once one of the largest industrial communities in Upper Canada. In 1801 Jonathan Morden built the first sawmill, and James Crooks (the origin of the name, Crooks' Hollow) harnessed the waterpower to establish a number of industries in the area along Crooks' Hollow Road and Spencer Creek.

From the parking lot going west, you will wander a short distance along a packed earth trail, and a shoreline with moss covered rocks and overhanging shrubs. You will approach a clearing at the present Christie Dam, where you can walk across the dam and begin the hike back toward the historical ruins and the village. From the Christie Dam you can still see remnants of Crooks' original stone dam.

Many decades ago there were 18 mills along Spencer Creek.

In 1812, Danley Mill supplied flour to the British Army. Its ruins are still standing.

Crooks' paper mill was built in 1826, the first such mill in Upper Canada (today known as Ontario), but it was destroyed by fire in 1875.

The swirling water rapids produce a quiet roar and a picturesque scene just before the raging water tumbles and falls into the creek below.

This loop trail is 1.5 km. At a moderate walk, and stopping for pictures and reading historical signs, it took us 45 minutes.

17
Chippewa Creek Trail:
Chippewa Creek Conservation Area

Difficulty: Beginner (great for children and the physically challenged)
Directions: QEW Highway Niagara bound, exit 57 at Victoria Ave. (Regional Rd. 24). Go south. Turn right onto Hwy. 20. Turn left at Regional Rd. 27 (Bismarck) and continue through Wellandport. Just after you cross the bridge over the Welland River, take the right fork and turn right on Regional Rd. 45. It's about an hour drive from Hamilton. Admission fees.

    The Chippewa Creek Conservation Area, where the Chippewa Creek Trail is located, consists of 148 hectares (366 acres) and includes a 14 hectare (35 acre) man-made reservoir called Dils Lake, camping facilities with 61 serviced lots, 40 campsites with no water or hydro and a special area for group camping. The camping area washrooms are equipped with hot showers, and firewood is available.
    Mid July, with the heat and humidity of summer is not always an ideal time to hike, but if the humidity is low and you have started out in the early morning, your danger of becoming overheated, or short of breath are greatly diminished. Choose a beginner trail near water when the temperatures are high, as the close proximity to water cools the air. Always take plenty of water to drink when you are hiking.
    Chippewa Creek Trail near Wellandport is ideal for hiking in summer conditions. The trail begins at a parking lot just before you enter the campsite area.

Only campers or visitors to the campsites are allowed past this point. Even though the temperature was soaring as we began our hike, we were lucky to have a brisk, north-easterly breeze skimming across Dils Lake. Because the trail is almost entirely in full sun, but skirts right at the edge of the water, we felt the full impact of the strong wind.

There are washroom facilities near the parking lot, just past the small, unsupervised beach, where there is a sign indicating: "No dogs allowed." Pets must be leashed at all times and not permitted in washrooms, water, or day use areas.

The trail begins to your right of the parking lot, at the boardwalk, and both are easy walking and wheelchair accessible. Stone dust makes up the surface of the trail, which travels around the entire perimeter of the lake.

All along the way you'll find many interesting combinations of open meadows and tree groves. Patches of water lilies with their spectacular white blooms swaying in rhythm to the movement of the water, created a white and green blanket on the water.

The lake habitats, wetlands and forest, attract waterfowl and birds. Wood ducks love to search the depth for water lily roots, while red-winged blackbirds are frequently seen swinging in the breeze on cattails.

Herons, with their long legs, prance quietly along the shore, hoping to catch a tasty meal of fish unaware of the danger lurking in the shallow waters.

Two fishing piers are also located here and are accessible to the physically challenged. As we passed the first pier, a short walk from the parking lot, a woman with two small children were trying their luck at fishing.

Suddenly, one of the children yelled excitedly, "I've got one, I've got one!" Remembering my childhood days when we thought that any little tug on the line was a fish, I smiled, expecting it was probably only a weed that he had hooked onto. My husband, out of curiosity, turned and looked back. Sure enough, a small fish still attached to the fishing line was flopping around on the floor of the pier.

Numerous fish species, such as large mouth bass, pike, sunfish and other related species are popular with anglers, young and old, here at Dils Lake. There is a boat ramp and access to the Welland River within the campgrounds, but no motorized boats are permitted on the lake.

The deep blue water sparkled like a field of diamonds in the bright morning sunlight, as we stopped to admire the view and take photographs. There are a number of narrow pathways out to the water's edge, where white-tailed deer cautiously come to drink just before dawn. Red fox, cottontail rabbits and coyotes have also been seen here, all a source of interest to hikers, outdoor photographers, wildlife enthusiasts and naturalists.

About midway around the lake, there is a large lookout platform with comfortable seating and a great panoramic view of the lake. A short distance from the platform is a floating dock, large picnic grounds with pavilion, and a designated area at the water's edge, where the canoe, paddleboat and kayak rentals are stored.

Taking the Chippewa Creek Trail, a leisurely 45-minute walk, is only part of the many things to do here. We ate our lunch at a shaded picnic table overlooking the lake, and began our hike back to the parking lot.

A number of swimmers were enjoying the cool freshness of the water, as we past the sandy beach. There is another parking lot at the picnic area just as you pass through the gatehouse.

Enjoying the sun at St. John's CA

18
St. John's Conservation Area
Sassafras Stroll:

Difficulty: Beginner
Directions: From the QEW Niagara bound, take exit 57 at Victoria Avenue (Regional Rd. 24). Proceed south to Hwy. #20 and turn left (east). At Pelham St. in Fonthill, turn north, which turns into Hollow Rd. At the cross roads of Barron Rd., and St. John's Rd., look for a conservation sign on your right. The trip will take approximately one hour from Hamilton.

St. John's Conservation Area is located within the Twelve Mile Creek Valley, which was formed by glaciers over thousand of years, when the ice retreated and advanced several times, eroding the soil and deepening the Twelve Mile Creek Valley.

In some places the Valley is filled with over 250 feet (76 metres) of glacial material and beneath lies buried the bedrock of the Niagara Escarpment.

After a week of high humidity and stifling hot temperatures, mid-July seemed to be the perfect time for a hike.

Sunny skies and a cool northerly breeze greeted us, as we emerged from our vehicle in a shaded parking lot at St. John's Conservation, near Fonthill. It was great to slip into my hiking boots again and I remember thinking that they were becoming as comfortable and familiar as a pair of old slippers. I slung on my backpack, slipped my arm through the camera strap then over my head to keep the camera steady as I walked, and made a stop at the washroom.

Every trail gets a thumbs-up from me if there is a washroom at the entrance. It's far more comfortable than hiding behind a bush or a tree.

Before we started the hike, we checked out all the information signs, including a map board and an excellent colour coded directory of the four trails, complete with the length of each trail and about how long it would take you to hike it. This kind of detailed information we had only seen once before at Crawford Lake, near Milton, and it proves to be extremely valuable. I only wish other trails would do the same.

I love being near water, so we decided to take the Sassafras Stroll, a 960-metre, 20-minute walk, colour coded in red, a loop that appeared to join the Pond Access Trail. The Sassafras Stroll got its name from the sassafras tree, unique to the Carolinian forest and found along this trail. It is sometimes referred to as the mitten tree as the leaves are three-lobed and mitten shaped. This trail begins at the far end of the parking lot near the colour-coded board and winds through a dense forest on a well-traveled path of hard- packed earth, tree roots and rocks.

Other species such as the tulip tree, flowering dogwood and butternut tree are also found lining the trail. A variety of ferns blanket the forest floor, along with over 400 species of vascular plants, which have been identified growing here in their natural setting.

A couple of boardwalks crossed swampy, bog-like areas and passed by a spring-fed pond, a former gravel pit. This small pond is used for rearing trout fingerlings to stock the main pond for the annual fishing season. "No Fishing" signs are posted here.

The relaxing walk through the coolness of the forest soon brings you out to a clearing and a 0.75-hectare (1.85 acre) picturesque trout pond.

We turned to the left on the Pond Access Trail and immediately spotted a turtle perched on a piece of log at the shore of an island centred near the end of the pond. It was an ideal picture-taking setting and I took full advantage. There was a bench along the path, a small wooden bridge and a sign indicating that while fishing was allowed, three fish was the maximum.

The pond area is the highlight of this hike. It was an absolute joy to walk along the shore on a stone dust path watching a family of geese that have resided there for many years and marvel at such a huge population of Painted Turtles. Often spotted here are other species of aquatic life and wildlife such as the Mallard Duck, Spring Peeper Frog, White-tailed Deer and songbirds. The island, logs, plants and fishing piers provide cover for the frogs, turtles and rainbow trout.

We felt as though we had just entered a secret garden known to very few. We shared this site with a young couple walking hand in hand, a lady with two children and a young woman with her morning coffee.

"Pedestrians Only" signs are posted on these trails. There are two wheelchair-accessible fishing piers, benches for sitting or enjoying a picnic, a lovely spot to fish or just sit and enjoy nature.

To reach this area without taking the hike through the forest, enter the tar path near the entrance to the parking lot. It is completely wheelchair and stroller accessible and a short walk. There's no admission, but there is a donation box at the tar path, near the pond. This did turn out to be a great day for a hike and a very pleasant experience. It is times like this that I feel I have a secret, that now has been shared with all of you, who drive along ribbons of highways everyday and unknowingly pass within minutes of this escape to peace and tranquility.

If you take the Sassafras Stroll ending at the Pond Access Trail and you have spent your time exploring the pond, the tar path will return you to the parking lot.

19
Bruce Trail at Smokey Hollow:

Difficulty: Advanced (hard packed earth, tree roots, rocks, and climbing)
Directions: From Hwy. 403 exit Hwy. 6 North. Turn right at Hwy. 5 and go east to Waterdown. Turn right (south) at traffic lights on Mill St. (Waterdown Rd). The parking lot is on your right, just past a railroad overpass. There are no washrooms. Free admission.

It was a hot and hazy early morning in July, when we slipped into the parking lot at Smokey Hollow, just off Mill St. in Waterdown. I love that name, Smokey Hollow. My mind conjures up all kinds of haunting stories, fictitious, but I'm sure if I delve deep enough, someone would come up with one to pique my interest.

But this is not a haunting place, especially in the morning sunlight. Although, just north a couple of blocks, the Waterdown Library has reportedly been haunted for years, but that's another story.

Smokey Hollow actually got its name from soot, dirt and smoke, air pollution emanating from a cluster of mills built around Waterdown Falls in the 1800's. Mind you, air pollution back then was a symbol of progress, something to be proud of. A flour mill was built by Henry Van Wagner of Albany, New York, for town founder, Ebenezer Culver Griffin. The story goes that as Henry sat gazing at waterfalls, he named his mill, Waterdown. Sadly, in 1912, a fire destroyed what was left of the booming industrial complex, by then doomed by the railroad's plan to bypass the town.
A section of the Bruce Trail begins here at the falls and meanders along scenic Grindstone Creek. From the

parking lot there are steps down to the edge of the gorge and then steel steps and platform take you farther down to the top of the falls. From here you experience the impressive depth, carved by glacier movement and the power it had to move huge slabs of rock, some absolutely breathtaking in size.

As you stand looking down at the falls, turn to your right, and you'll find the only evidence that anything was ever built here: Two stone structures, one on either side of the creek. It appears to have been a foundation for a water wheel. The best time to view the falls is in the spring, when the volume of water is at its peak, but water cascading over the falls is visible anytime of the year and picture perfect in winter.

As you begin the trail there is a bench, where you get a view of the falling water through the trees. Because of the leaves in summer, getting a clear view for photography can put you somewhere where you aren't suppose to be. Remember, going to the edge can be exciting. But going over the edge can be downright embarrassing, if you live to tell it.

A short distance along, the trail, turns to follow the creek, where a number of hard packed earth and wooden stairs descend to the creek below, drawing you into a natural wonderland of sights, sounds and smells. Nature, somehow, has a way of letting you know what a small part you play in this evolving world of ours, and sitting on a slab of rock as big as your backyard puts this all in prospective. There are many stairs and rocks to climb along this trail. Some parts are easy walking, while others demand a degree of cardiac ability and muscle performance. Along the way two snakes slithered across our path. Up ahead, a skunk waddled and disappeared into the foliage. A friendly chipmunk scampered beside us on a fallen log.

Against our better judgment, we took this trail on a hot, humid day. Our destination, westward, on a stretch of the Bruce Trail from Smokey Hollow to Highway #6, documented to be 4.8 km (3 miles).

The knowledge of distance before you start a trail is always helpful, but it can sometimes distort your sense of the time that is required to complete the hike. On a straight flat surface it wouldn't demand much effort, but you tend to forget the time needed for climbing, uphill/downhill grades, and winding trails.

We arrived at a bridge crossing Grindstone Creek in about an hour. Here, because of the rising heat and humidity, we thought of turning back, but I wanted to complete the hike over to Highway #6, and I really thought it was probably just around the next bend.

After leaving the bridge on the valley floor, we started a steady uphill climb, winding along the sloping face of the escarpment, now and then hoping to hear a hint of traffic noise that would indicate we were nearing the highway. Our energy level was dropping fast as we moved forward in the heat. With half of our water supply gone, and no breeze to give any relief, we decided for safety's sake, to turn back.

When we returned to the parking lot at Smokey Hollow, we had hiked a total of three hours, and after extensive analysis, comparing Highway #5 as a guide, we were shocked to learn that we had only covered one third of that stretch of the Bruce Trail. We quickly learned that day that hiking in hot humid weather changes your physical abilities and we had forgotten to be cautious about thinking that the end of the trail is just over the hill, or around the next bend.

A couple we met on our return trip thought it was just a casual hike over to Hwy. #6. With no water or food and our tale of discovery, they turned back. The length of time to travel any trail is only known by one who has done it, and most of us are not privy to that information. From Smokey Hollow to the bridge is a wonderful hike. It should take about two hours, return.

20
F.W.R. Dickson Wilderness Trail:

Difficulty: Beginner (hard-packed earth, tree roots)
Directions: Take Hwy. 403 west to Hwy. 24 North. Go north through Brantford, turn left at the traffic light at Hwy 5 and head west into Paris. In Paris, take Hwy 24A North and turn left (west) on Brant-Waterloo Rd. Watch carefully for a faded sign for F.W.R. Dickson Wilderness on your right. If you just want to go to Bannister Lake and observation tower, stay on Hwy. 24A a short distance, turn left (west) on Regional Rd. 49. The parking lot is on the right. Both areas are an hour drive from Hamilton. Free admission.

Have you ever dreamed of traveling to a jungle, wielding a machete as you thrashed through bug invested terrain, crossed swamps and pushed through high grasses taller than your sweaty armpits? Well, slap on that bug repellent and pull on long pants for protection, because we have it right here in Ontario at F.W.R. Dickson Wilderness Trail, just north of Paris.

I know, you probably think the heat and humidity has pushed me over the edge, but in late July the humid air had dissipated and it was a perfect day for a hike. The trail begins at a parking lot off Brant-Waterloo Rd where there is a covered shelter, a map showing 84 acres of nature trails, and two signs indicating "Dogs must be on a leash," and "Leave no litter, take only pictures." There are no washrooms or picnic tables.

The trail heads north, through an open meadow filled with wild pink Beebalm. It was astonishing to see these and other wild flowers had survived the heat and lack of rainfall that plagued us for weeks. Within a short distance from the parking lot you'll climb wood and earth stairs. Follow the path and descend down to the right on a number of wooden steps that will lead you to a boardwalk over a large swampy area.

Water plants are so dense here that some have grown over the walkway, obscuring all visible signs of water, or creatures, living in its slimy depths. This environment is ideal for a number of bug species to thrive. On the railing sat a bug resembling a housefly in shape, but about half the size of a hummingbird, shiny black, with a wing span of 10 cm. (4 inches) I was very close, but when I tried to take his picture he crawled under the railing out of view, then flew away.

Traveling over hard-packed earth and tree roots you will pass through patches of thick bush and grass, until you come to a large slime green pond. From here you have a choice of taking the path to the left, around the pond perimeter and head back, (an hour hike), or keep to the right and continue as we did to Wrigley Lake. After crossing another meadow of tall grasses, there is a wooden sign pointing to the lake, and caution to continue only at your own risk. Of course we did.

Here, the path gets interesting: Underbrush so thick you can't see ahead of you, thorns, thistles, shoulder high weeds, dragon flies, black horseflies larger than bumble bees and clouds of the dreaded mosquitoes, so thick that opening your mouth was dangerous. We thought a machete would have been useful at this point, and although I am not intimidated by this kind of environment and unafraid of anything smaller than me, I was beginning to wonder what could be lurking in the tall grass. While I was imagining we were actually on safari, we rounded a bend with me in the lead. As I glanced up, something elephant sized and white shone through the brush. I did a stutter step and then realized it was just an old dead tree bleached white by the sun, its large branches bent and spread out like octopus arms. We paused to explore it.

Soon the trail opened up, and we arrived at Wrigley Lake. It's a shallow lake, where no watercraft is allowed. Water lilies, and lush ferns give a pleasant view, as the trail meanders through trees. Sumac trees were in groves along the way, giving the environment a tropical look. Wild raspberries, and blackberries were in abundance. As we sampled a few, we were surprised to find both varieties much sweeter than domestic ones.

Beauty was unbelievably dispersed along the path. Delicate pink flowers on long thin stems draped over the trail. Beautiful yellow trumpet-like flowers dotted a vine that entwined anything in its path. Even shoulder-high thistles showed off blooms of vibrant pink. We found a multitude of spring flowers, which had long since met their demise, and made a mental note to recommend this trail for springtime hiking.

After leaving Wrigley Lake, the trail continues north until it crosses Regional Rd. 49, with another parking lot and trail into Bannister Lake, where an observation tower to view springtime, migrating birds is located. Here we noticed a large family of baby ducks. The steel constructed observation tower is extremely high and allows full view of the lake.

After leaving the tower there is a small loop that will return you to the main trail. You cannot get lost. There are no other trails until you return past Wrigley Lake and back to the first pond. The pond is clearly visible from the path. Keep to your right and follow the trail around the pond and back to the parking lot.

The round trip is three miles and took us about two and a half hours. There are a few stairs to provide easy walking up and down inclines, but the trail is mostly flat. We were alone on this trail with only the croaking of frogs to keep us company.

The Grand River

21
Paris To Cambridge Rail Trail and Paris Dam:

Difficulty: Beginner (hard packed gravel, flat surface)
Directions: From Hamilton, take Hwy. 403 West to Hwy. 24 North. Continue North through Brantford, turn left onto Hwy 5 and head west into Paris. Turn right on Willow Street (just before the bridge over the Grand River). Follow this a short distance and the parking lot for Paris Dam is on your left. The parking lot for the trail is further up Willow, also on your left. Both areas are about 40 minutes from Hamilton.

There is no admission to the Paris Dam, but there is an honorary collection box at the entrance to the Paris to Cambridge Rail-Trail. Dogs must be leashed.

The Grand River Conservation Authority opened this stretch of trail in 1994, and was the first to convert an abandoned rail line for recreational use in southern Ontario. It follows the roadbed of the old Lake Erie & Northern Railway passing through the Carolinian Grand River Forest and extends 18 km (11 miles).

Although we only hiked as far as Glen Morris, about midway to Cambridge, it was an easy walking surface with wonderful summertime views of the Grand River. I took photographs of canoeists shouting with joy as they fought the strong current, carrying them swiftly along the shallow waters to Paris. In springtime, this river over flows its banks, and widens with the large volume of water.

The Paris to Cambridge Rail-Trail is part of the Trans Canada Trail, an extensive trail system that links Hamilton, Brantford and Cambridge in an 80 km (50 mile) loop in southern Ontario. There are signs, marking off the kilometres on the way to Cambridge and at kilometre 15.9, there is a series of stairs leading you up to a large cement platform overlooking the Grand River. From the parking lot in Paris to this point is about a 50-minute walk.

We found that this stretch of trail is the most scenic. Although we continued on and located a picturesque view of the river, and found benches at kilometre 12, most of the trail to that point was just a great hike with only short glimpses of the river through the trees. It also passes through open meadows, and the heat of a blazing August sun was taking its toll on us. Benches are located here and throughout the trail.

All along were remnants of wildflowers remaining in bloom even after a lack of rainfall. Most abundant were groups of Black-eyed Susans standing erect on stems approximately three feet high. There was also a smattering of Bouncing Bets with their pink blooms that constantly remind me of the smell of black liquorice. Mosquitoes swarmed in shade and standing water. But bug repellent always does the trick.

This is a multi-purpose trail, ideal for wheelchairs (except at lookouts), cyclists, runners, hikers and cross-country skiers. No motorized vehicles and no camping or open fires are permitted. Staying to the right is always a good practice on a multi-purpose trail to allow faster users the right of way. This avoids being frightened by a cyclist who has failed to give you a passing warning. I have been known to scream, probably frightening the wild life, while enjoying a quiet woodlands hike, when one has approached at top speed seeming to come out of no where.

Everyone we met on this trail was friendly and courteous, complete with smile and greeting, adding to the enjoyment of the hike, but we found that we had overextended ourselves with the distance we covered in the heat of the summer. On our return trip from Glen Morris back to the parking lot in Paris, we had covered approximately 18 km (11 miles).

I would not recommend this trail for those of you who would like a challenge, climbing rocks and hills.

The challenge here is in the length of trail you want to cover. It is an exercise trail, with the added interest of viewing the Grand River.

Sometimes the best is left to last: The Paris Dam. isn't part of this trail. It belongs to a connecting trail called SC Johnson Trail leading into Brantford.

But I'm including the Paris Dam with this hike because you pass the parking lot for the Paris Dam, on your way to the parking lot for the Paris to Cambridge Rail-Trail and you must take the time to stop and see it. This dam is the source of water supply for the City of Brantford. There is limited parking for the dam, especially on weekends, but get there early or arrive during the week and there should not be a problem.

There's a set of wooden stairs leading up to the path, if you would rather not climb the hill. But I recommend climbing the hill if at all possible.

A spectacular view is yours after you climb the hill, a grass embankment leading to an open path and lookout.

Photographers will enjoy the many angles available to shoot the falls, unimpeded by trees or shrubbery.

Just at the top of the falls there's a lookout, where the water, incredibly, resembles black glass and appears not to be moving. It is a sensational experience, and one not to be missed.

22
Hilton Falls Trail:

Difficulty: Beginner to Intermediate
Directions: Hwy. 401 to Guelph Line North (exit 312) to Campbellville Rd. east to the park entrance. From QEW, take Guelph Line North (exit 102) to Campbellville Rd. east to park entrance. Entry fee.

It was late August. Threatening skies promised rain, but a moderate breeze kept the humidity at a comfortable level. At first we debated whether to begin the hike, but with our rain gear packed, why not?

Four trails are at Hilton Falls Conservation Area near Campbellville, Ont. Hilton Falls Trail is colour-coded in yellow, Red Oak Trail in red, Bent Rim Biking Trail in green and Beaver Dam Trail in orange. The Information Center has washrooms, brochures, and picnic tables. The trail begins a short distance off, up a steep incline, with excellent walking on crushed stone. For our hike, we chose the Hilton Falls Trail to view the falls, take photos, and eat our picnic lunch.

It was early morning. Few hikers had ventured out, but some cyclists passed by, waving greetings. A short distance into our hike, the sun emerged from the clouds, raising the humidity to uncomfortable level. The breeze had picked up and was certainly welcomed. Without it, the air would have been stifling.

About 40 minutes along an easy walking trail, we arrived at the falls area. A blackened fire-pit with a supply of firewood dominated a clearing, with seating, picnic tables and stairs leading down to the base of the falls. As you stand on the lookout, above you is a huge overhang of solid rock with interesting moss formations and trickling water. Mist from the falls creates a rain-forest environment, alive with interesting foliage. Across the creek bed, stands the brick ruins of three 19th century sawmills and the stone framing that once supported a huge waterwheel. An archway had been constructed many years ago, in the front wall of the structure to provide an exit for the water that turned the 40-foot diameter wheel, and to allow the water to flow back into the Sixteen Mile Creek.

The first sawmill was constructed by Edward Hilton in 1835. In 1837 he left for the United States and the saw mill fell into disrepair. In 1856, George Park acquired the land, and the mill again became operational. He sold it in 1857, and it was destroyed by fire in 1860. Little is known about the third mill. Constructed by John Richards, it operated from 1863 to 1867, when it too burned down.

It had been a very dry summer. Water was still cascading over the falls, but the rocky creek bed was virtually dry. We walked across, and climbed onto the stone water wheel support structure and ate lunch. A few feet away, water fell 10 meters to the creek below. Here, the rich environment supports a variety of plant and animal species. Hilton Falls is a major breeding sites for the West Virginia white butterfly. The larval food supply, the toothwort plant, is rarely found in Ontario. Yellow Lady's Slipper can also be found here in spring. Birds include the Nashville Warbler, and there are spotted salamanders. Soon it was time to leave this magical place, where a curious mind and photographer's eyes are nature's puppets.

The trail back has a loop that guides you through mature trees, passes over the main trail to the falls, and brings you back to the information centre. The Hilton Falls Trail is easy walking, (four km,) with very little upgrade climbing. Taking time for lunch and photos, it took us two hours.

Rock Formation at Buffalo Craig Trail

23
Buffalo Craig Trail
and Vista Adventure Trail:

Difficulty: Beginner (incline and stair climbing, rocks and tree roots), distance 1.5 km.
Directions: From the QEW exit at Appleby Line in Burlington, go north on Appleby about 10 km, just past Derry Road. Watch for the Rattlesnake Point Conservation sign on your left. There is an admission fee. Annual Passes are available and group camping is available by permit. No alcohol, bicycles or vehicles are permitted. Maps are provided at the gatehouse.

You really don't have to spend a lot of time on long hikes to find unusual rock formations, 30 species of flowers and foliage, turkey vultures, bats, deer, fox, raccoons and porcupines. All you have to do is spend at least an hour hiking a portion of the Buffalo Craig Trail and the Vista Adventure Trail that together form a loop at Rattlesnake Point Conservation Area. In fact, this short hike includes one of the most spectacular views in Ontario.

These trails are located within 727 acres of sheer cliffs, crevice caves, talus slopes and glacial deposits.

It's all part of Ontario's Niagara Escarpment, which runs from Queenston, near Niagara Falls to the very tip of the Bruce Peninsula at Tobermory, a distance of approximately 725 km.

Formed over 400 million years ago by a gigantic tropical sea, the Niagara Escarpment breaks here to form Lowville Valley, which lies between Rattlesnake

Point, and Mount Nemo to the east. Far below lies a patchwork quilt of countryside and breathtaking views of the Toronto skyline, Oakville, Lake Ontario, Mount Nemo, and Burlington. We have been on long hikes and have never seen more spectacular vistas as this 1.5 km (about a mile) trail provides.

As we left the gatehouse at the park entrance, we kept to our right, driving a short distance along a gravel road. Soon we arrived at a large parking lot, complete with washroom facilities, picnic gazebo and large picnic area. Park at this location and proceed to your left along the roadway. In a few minutes, you will see trail markings of yellow, blue and red on a trail entering the forest on your left. Follow that trail as you climb a steep incline consisting of hard packed earth, tree roots and rocks, and at the top you will find a gravel road. Turn to the right and follow the gravel road to another parking area.

Here, we found a family of raccoons scouring a dumpster for a delicate tidbit for an early morning breakfast. They are so cute in the wild with their little beady eyes, but in your backyard they can be masked bandits, as their natural markings depict. Not wanting human company, and probably knowing they were in a place where they were not suppose to be, they quickly climbed a nearby tree, all the while looking down at us with an innocent stare. They didn't stick around for a photo. It was one of those great shots that got away.

The red markings, trail map and the beginning of the Vista Adventure Trail begin here at the parking lot and enter a wooded area along an easy walking trail.

In a few minutes, you will come to a set of metal stairs that take you down to the Pinnacle Lookout, a towering rock that appears to have broken away from the main rock face to stand alone. It's somewhat intimidating in size and you feel a sense of wonderment about what on earth is keeping it from tumbling down into the valley below.

As you ascend the stairs back to the original trail, turn to your right and at the end of this short path is the Trafalgar Lookout. Here you can see as far as the skyline of Toronto and all points in between. After you have pulled yourself away from this awesome view, return to the stairs and continue on the original trail marked in red, the Vista Adventure Trail.

This trail continues along the very edge of the escarpment with plenty of lookouts and if you are lucky, you may come across some climbers, as we did. We saw their ropes tied off on a couple of trees and could hear their voices, but they were far below climbing down the escarpment face. I tried to get a glimpse of them as they rappelled down the steep embankment, but there were no clear angles to capture them in my viewfinder for a photograph, and I had already gone closer to the edge than I should have.

A wide variety of climbing grades makes Rattlesnake Point one of the most popular areas to rock climb in Ontario. Cliff heights range from 30 to 80 feet. The first party of persons to record a new climb has the honour of naming it. Examples include: Creepy Crawly, Space Case, Holy Cow and After You. High risk is involved, so experience is a must.

All along the escarpment there are signs posted, warning of loose and unstable rock, which is not unusual when you are hiking anywhere on the Niagara Escarpment. The rock is especially dangerous when wet, or covered in fallen leaves.

This Vista Adventure Trail, marked with a red circle and arrow, will take you back to the parking lot, where you parked your vehicle. Here you can spend the day having a picnic in the pavilion or lunch around a large fire-pit. A great way to close off an enjoyable hiking experience.

24
Bruce Trail at Kern's Road:

Difficulty: Intermediate/advanced (Incline climbing, rocks, tree roots)
Directions: From Hamilton, take Hwy. 6 north. Turn right (east) on Hwy. 5 through Waterdown. Watch for Kern's Rd. on your right. Follow Kern's Rd. down a hill, along an S bend. The parking lot is on your right.

If you have never taken a hike on the Bruce Trail, or if you are a frequent visitor and would like to share a wonderful experience with your family and friends, this section of the Bruce Trail is a great place to start.

It has many of the elements you can expect to find on any portion of the Bruce Trail, which stretches from Niagara Falls in the south, to Tobermory in the north, a distance of approximately 800 km. (1,287.4 miles).

On a bright, early summer morning in August, we laced up our hiking boots, hoisted our backpacks on and checked our map. Since we are first-time visitors on all the trails I profile, we never know what to expect. And so, with keen curiosity and the thrill of adventure, we left the parking lot on Kerns Rd., just east of Waterdown and began our hike.

There is parking for a few cars along the road at the trail entrance, but just follow the S-bend down the hill and on your right is a large parking lot. From there you get a preview of the wonderful panoramic views you will experience along this trail.

After leaving the parking lot, hike back up the hill and on your right, the trail markings will lead you into a wooded lot filled with maple, oak, and hickory trees. Visiting this trail in September or October would be a perfect time to experience all the fall colours, as you scuff through fallen leaves and breathe the cool autumn air. A few minutes into your hike, you'll see steel railings on the edge of a large stone quarry, and from here a full view of Hamilton, Burlington, Toronto, and Lake Ontario is spread out before you. The sun shining on Lake Ontario at 8:30 in the morning gave off a spectacular glare and spotlighted the valley against the brilliant, clear blue of the sky. Panoramic vistas can be photographed in many locations along this stretch.

Soon, the trail leads down a steep rocky descent, into a wooded valley. Just stand for a moment before you make the descent and look down at the wonder of nature. Even in August, with no fall colours, the view from the top caused us to pause and admire the fresh green and sculptured neatness of the valley floor.

Nowhere, sitting in your vehicles driving along at break-neck speeds, can you ever experience this natural beauty until you get out and walk.

You will need a degree of hiking ability to navigate this trail, but it is not exceptionally difficult, unless you have been leading a sedentary life. A good pair of well-fitting hiking boots with ankle supports would be advisable. Here I can give you the best tip, guaranteed to avoid getting blisters on your feet. Wear a good pair of ladies nylon knee-highs or anklets under your sport socks. If you wear the knee-highs fold them down to your ankles so they won't cut off any circulation to your calf muscles. The guys can do this too – no one will ever know.

We crossed a bridge over a stream that we imagined would be full of fast flowing water in springtime. But in the heat of the summer with a lack of rainfall, it was nearly dry. We noticed remnants of flowers, such as large patches of columbine and leaves of other species that had long since returned to the earth, with only a promise to appear again after the melting of the winter snowfall. The purple Beebalm was still in bloom and a yellow daisy-like flower raised its head proudly on long stems. If you are very quiet, a rustle could mean a chipmunk, a squirrel, and or even a raccoon, like the one we saw scurry into a hollow log to avoid our company.

In about 50 minutes you will arrive at Hwy. 5 (Dundas St.), a busy four-lane highway. The stretch that you have now just covered is the most scenic.

We continued on toward Guelph Line, crossing Hwy. 5 to a gravel road, where on your right, you will see the white, painted rectangles, familiar signs of the Bruce Trail. On this portion of the trail, we had our first experience at stile climbing. A stile is a wooden ladder built over an existing fence. I am not brave at climbing ladders or fences. As a matter of fact, living in the country as a child, my friends would nimbly clear the top of my Grandfather's page wire fencing without a scratch, while I'd promptly, with the grace of a beached whale, fall over it. Needless to say, I was a bit apprehensive as we approached the first stile.

There are three stiles along this trail: One just as you cross Hwy. 5, and one on either side of Cedar Springs Rd. After crossing here, the trail continues east to Guelph Line, through private woodlots and farmland. From Hwy 5 to Guelph Line is about a one-hour-and-10-minute hike. On our return trip, having to cross those three stiles once more, I felt like an expert, and navigated over them with control and grace.

The trip beginning at Kern's Rd. to the Guelph Line and your return, is about 9.8 km (6 miles), and took us four hours. We were hot and tired when we arrived back at the parking lot on Kern's Rd.

But there was a cool breeze blowing out of the north as we sat large under a old tree, ate our lunch, slipped off our boots and freely wriggled our toes.

It was a great day

25
Lakeshore Lookout Trail
Mountsberg Conservation Area:

Difficulty: Beginner (flat surface – Stairs to lookout towers)
Directions: From the QEW, take Guelph Line North (exit 102) and go west on Campbellville Rd, and north on Milborough Line to the park entrance. Watch for signs. It's about 30 minutes from downtown Hamilton. Trails traverse protected conservation lands. Hikers use trails at own risk. Pets must be leashed. Vehicles are prohibited. An admission fee applies.

The first week in September brought along a brisk northerly breeze that had been lightly kissed by fall. It graciously reminded me that winter was not far behind.

I hate winter. With the chill in the air, my mood was just under the weather – or was it the argument I just had had with my computer, which was waiting for me at home?

As I exited our vehicle my mind was still on the computer. And I wondered why on earth I was letting a machine create so much frustration.

My mood was soon to be lifted and the stress washed away as we began our hike.

Lakeshore Lookout Trail is near Campbellville, in the Mountsberg Conservation Area, one of five parks under Conservation Halton authority. Mountsberg Conservation is famous for the springtime maple syrup festival, but wild life also flourishes here. Bald eagles, red-tailed hawks, great horned owls, and more than

218 other species of birds have been seen and recorded in the area by the conservation authorities.

There are five separate trails branching out from the Visitor's Center and herds of Elk and Bison can be viewed on the Wildlife Walkway Trail, roaming a fenced off area provided especially for them.

Everyone can pet and feed the farm animals, and are fish the 200-hectare lake. Or, they can hike, cycle, or ski 16 km of trails. The Visitor Center has maps, souvenirs, wildlife displays of the many animals found in the conservation area (including Red Fox), teaching facilities and washrooms. There is a raptor centre with exhibits, live birds to view, and rehabilitation facilities for sick and injured birds of prey.

The Lakeshore Lookout Trail, marked with a blue circle and arrow, is 5.6 km. (3.5 miles), and took us two and half hours. That time included taking photos, climbing two lookout towers, examining foliage/trees, and discovering rock piles, the former foundations of abandoned homes and barns crumbled from age.

At the beginning of the trail you pass over a rail line, which has warning signs posted, making sure you are aware that a train could arrive at any time, so look and listen before crossing. There is also a map board, with the name of all the trails, the length of each one and how much time it might require to complete the hike. This information in my estimation is invaluable.

Along the way, an old abandoned barn was sending a sad reminder of the passing of time. It provided a picturesque setting, partially covered with the wild growth patterns of vines engulfing its walls, holding the green of the leaves as a beautiful contrast against the rusted steel exterior.

A short way into your hike you will arrive at Swallowville, a name given to a row of bird houses making up a colony for 150 tree swallows, which dart along the shoreline during the months of May and June. Herons search for fish at the water's edge and osprey glide over the lake hoping for a tasty fish.

We found some unusual and delicate orange and yellow flowers called "Spotted Touch-me-nots". They can grow between two and five feet high with a flower only one inch across. It always amazes me how something that delicate can survive in the wild.

My Grandfather pointed these out to me on his farm when I was a child, and his memory came flooding back to me as if it only happened yesterday. "Come," he would say, "Watch this," as he would, oh so very gently, touch his finger to a seed pod and it would pop and burst open with such force I'd jump back in surprise.

It even surprised me again today, as I showed my husband what my grandfather had taught me. My grandfather was a great teacher and my understanding and love of nature has come from him.

The trail was easy walking, on a relatively flat surface of hard-packed earth and gravel, trampled grass and tree roots.

There are a number of stairs at the wooden constructed lookout towers, where there is a clear view of the lake at two different locations, but I was disappointed to find that when actually hiking on the trail, the lake was hardly visible through the trees.

Grapevines with their late harvest of green and purple grapes also reminded us that fall was nipping at our heels and I gave a little shiver.

I would recommend this trail as a springtime hike, when the migrating birds would be plentiful and the wild flowers would create colourful interest.

In fact, in one location there was a large grove of lilac bushes and at the right time of the year, probably June, the sight and smell would be a nice treat after a long winter.

Eight-sided school house

26
Backus Heritage Village Trail:

Difficulty: Beginner.
Directions: Hwy. 403, then Hwy. 24 South, through the city of Simcoe. Turn left on Regional Rd. 16, then right on Regional Rd. 42, and follow the signs to the Conservation Area. Admission is by contribution.

A light breeze and sunny skies in late September set the scene for our leisurely hike through this heritage village, just north of Port Rowan, Ontario.

Gravel and grass paths made the walk accessible to everyone; a great way to spend the day exploring our past. Wheelchair accessible restrooms are located in Conservation Education Centre, Heritage Building, and pool change rooms. Pick up a map of the village at the park entrance. There are also picnic areas, swimming pool and a 160-site campground.

You get the feeling you've come to visit an old friend, when you enter the family home: The table is set for dinner, and the rooms furnished with precious artefacts. For a moment, I thought I could taste Grandma's apple pie. Take a rest on the front porch that overlooks the pond and reflect back to a time when you might have visited your grandparents' old country home. I could smell hay from the nearby barn and remembered my grandfather throwing hay to the cows.

There are 12 kilometres of nature trails crossing 850 acres. Most contain sandy ridges, swamps, forests and a wide variety of plants and animals. A duck-hunting contest was being held on the pond, the day we arrived, complete with hunters, duck decoys, canoes, wooden boats, and contest officials.

The Backus Heritage Conservation Area village has 29 specific areas in which you can discover and explore barns, sawmill, museum, Backus gravestones, Backus homestead, blacksmith shop, corncrib, militia log cabin, Teeterville Baptist Church built in 1869, and a log house. The most interesting for me was the Cherry Valley Schoolhouse, which was relocated to the village in 1982. It was moved there from its original site on Cherry Valley Road near Waterford, Ontario. This unusual, octagon-shaped school was originally built in 1866, and is one of only two known octagonal-shaped schools to have been built in Ontario. The original wooden benches are now standing alone, in rows, as though waiting for the clamber of students and the ringing of the big brass school bell.

John C. Backhouse was known as the first person to implement preservation of forests using management techniques. He did this using sleds, skids, and horse teams for hauling. He only cut diseased or damaged trees. He supplied lumber from the woodlot bordering the village, to rebuild the Welland Canal. He also sent large white pines to England for British Navy ship masts. Logging continued here to the mid-20th century.

We ate lunch in a clearing, perched on a giant log, which had been worn smooth with the seats of frequent visitors to a nearby campfire pit. Through the trees, the murky water of the pond glistened and the sun filtered through the trees. A Blue Jay screamed and flew overhead, perhaps scolding us for disrupting his private sanctuary. It is interesting to check out the aquatic life around the pond, enjoy a picnic lunch under a shade tree, take a swim in the pool, or just relax for a few days at the campgrounds.

If you're looking for a hiking trail with scenic views and want major cardio exercise, this is not the place. But it does offer a wonderful walk through an historical village.

27
Black Creek Side Trail:

Difficulty: Intermediate/Advanced (some climbing, hard-packed earth, tree roots, rocks)
Directions: From QEW in Oakville, take Hwy 25 North through Milton, crossing over Hwy. 401, to the 15th Sideroad. Turn right (east) and travel to the 5th Line and turn left (north). Follow the 5th line until you come to a ball park on your right. There is plenty of parking. It is well worth the trip and a great drive in the country. There is no admission fee.

The enjoyment we encountered as we explored the Black Creek Trail, a side link to the Bruce Trail in the Limehouse Conservation Area, west of Georgetown, is etched in my mind as a truly fascinating experience. The trail begins in a ballpark on the 5th Line, where a blue sign and painted rectangles of a link to the Bruce Trail are clearly marked. The only washroom facility is located here.

Late September gave us ideal weather for hiking. The sun pushed its way through the clouds, a cool breeze meandered through the pines and the musty smell of damp earth and wood let you know that you were in the lap of nature.

A torrential rain the day before left the air still moist and fresh, and gave an unusual look to the forest. It was an eerie blackness, like a whimsical picture you might see in a storybook. The rain, as it traveled down the outer layer of the trees, had turned the bark from the natural grey to black. The most dramatic were the white birch, where rain had soaked the inner wood in bare spots and created a dramatic effect. This ghostly feeling was transformed as you looked skyward, and saw the green leaves of the hickory, oak, beech and ash, along with the pines, swaying in the sunlight.

A thick carpet of pine needles softened our steps, and the silence was almost deafening. We were alone. The birds were quiet and the wildlife stayed hidden, although we somehow knew they were there. Hollowed out logs, created by a furry resident for a winter shelter, let me know that the cold and snow would soon be upon us.

About halfway through the loop, the trail leads down to the Black Creek. After the heavy rainfall we had had the previous day, it was running full and fast. Although the trail leads through the forest right down to the banks of the creek, the trees open to a spacious location with a pine needle carpeting, and a high ceiling of foliage. Almost like a room with a view.

The trail is easy to follow, as long as you watch for the blue painted rectangles that will lead you along the path. Sometimes, you are so fascinated by the landscape that you forget to locate those markings, but you must, at all times, stop, and know where you are. Across the path, a tree had fallen to its death, and like a giant serpent, laid arched and twisted, a green moss skin clinging to its back.

The trail follows along the creek, until you come to a trail leading off to the left. Follow the path past this point as far as the wooden bridge over the creek. Here you'll see a wall and a half circle of stone built ages ago, perhaps part of an old mill or waterwheel. This is a great place for photographs.

But the best is yet to come.

Turn and go back to the first trail you just passed and take the trail to the right. The terrain becomes more rugged, and the moss-covered rocks bigger, and you begin to feel how small you are as you climb upward over crevices so deep you can't see the bottom. You climb higher and suddenly it levels off, but right in front of you the trail leads you through, "The Hole in the Wall." It is a name given to a narrow opening in the rock face, and the most fascinating part of the hike.

As you pass through this narrow opening, there is a wooden ladder taking you up to the next level. From here, you can look down into a deep passage in the rock. Children and pets must be watched closely at all times when hiking, but especially here. One false move and you could find yourself at the bottom of one of those deep caverns.

Another ladder takes you up to the second level, and now you can look down and experience the full impact of what you have just come through. As I continued to photograph, I realized that I was trying to capture the feeling of this unusual place and had to remind myself that photos are only tools to remind us. It took me several minutes to tear myself away, reluctant to leave it all behind.

Here the trail is harder to find if you are not watching for the Bruce Trail markings on the trees. You are walking on solid rock with a carpet of pine needles and deep cracks, so a well-traveled path is not clearly evident. Trees grow in the most unusual contortions, forever fighting to find soil they need for life. Roots protrude from the crevices, and then, somehow, turn and disappear back into the rock. These trees are hundreds of years old, and I still find it amazing they have survived. Soon you are back at the park, where you parked your vehicle.

We stopped to have lunch at a picnic table, and somehow felt just a little disappointed to be back from the world we left behind. Our hike was approximately a 2.8 km. (1 ½ miles) loop, took us one hour and 45 minutes – and it will forever be noted as one of our most unforgettable hikes.

The Battlefield Monument

28

The Devil's Punch Bowl
on The Bruce Trail:

Difficulty: Advanced (some difficult climbing)
Directions: From the QEW Niagara, take exit at Centennial Parkway (Hwy. 20). Turn right off the ramp and travel five minutes to King St. E. Turn left and immediately watch for the sign for Battlefield Park on you right. There is no admission fee at either park.

From the beginning to end of this trail, you'll see the comparison between the spectacular architecture made by human hands, and the astonishing and unbelievable spectacle created by the hands of nature.

We began our hike at Battlefield Park in Stoney Creek. Today, it's a grand garden with a monument reaching hundreds of feet into the air. This monument reminds us that a violent battle took place on June 4, 1813 where an invading American army of around 3,000 camped nearby. Under cover of darkness, 700 British Regulars executed a surprise attack the next morning. It was a violent battle with heavy losses on both sides. But the Americans were defeated and withdrew. The victory is credited with saving Upper Canada from being overrun in 1813.

When you first enter Battlefield Park, you will see a large white house that has been moved approximately half a kilometre from its original site at the corner of King St. and Nash Road. When Mrs. Leone Jackson passed away in 1996, the Jackson family donated the house to the City of Stoney Creek. The house was built in 1810, and played a role in the Battle of Stoney

Creek in June of 1813. At that time it was used as a field hospital. There are plans for it to become a Tea Room, Gift Shop, and rental space for seminars, weddings and other social functions.

As you look beyond the house, steps lead up to the enormous monument situated in a gorgeous setting of trees and flowers. As you follow the roadway around the building, you will come to a huge parking lot with a picnic area and washroom facilities. Walk across the grassy area and a blue sign depicting the link to the Bruce Trail is posted there.

Take this path for about 20 minutes and you will come to an often used railroad. Before crossing the track, turn to your left, and walk a short distance until you see a Bruce Trail sign posted on a tree on the other side of the railway tracks. Be extremely cautious, as the traffic sounds from Centennial Parkway can drown out an approaching train. Cross the tracks and head into the forest and follow the trail to the left. In about a half an hour you will see the railway tracks again, but do not cross. Follow the Bruce Trail to the right down into the valley and look up. You are now at the bottom of The Devil's Punch Bowl.

When we were there mid September there was no water cascading down over the layers of rock, but in springtime it must be a vision not to be missed. Off to the left is a set of earth and wooden stairs. Follow the steps up to a level about half way up the escarpment, where again you will see a sign indicating a Bruce Trail Link to the top of the Devil's Punch Bowl. Here the trail gets more difficult: It's a steep climb on loose stones and hard packed earth, with no tree roots or trees to allow a handhold. But the spectacular view at the top is well worth the effort. A large cement lookout is located in a park setting and produces the breathtaking view of Hamilton and Lake Ontario. As you walk along the edge of the park, you get the full impact of the depth and the circular construction of the Devil's Punch Bowl. Nature's hands have precisely carved out a gigantic bowl. Millions of years ago, this round pit was cut and moulded by the swirling of many different sizes of stones under the tremendous power generating by the melting of glacier waters. Like a giant washing machine, it drove the rocks around and around, cutting away the rock, until it formed this gigantic hole. It seems like a bottomless pit, and there are many tales about what might be down there.

The escarpment has been designated a world biosphere reserve by UNESCO (the United Nations Educational, Scientific, and Cultural Organization). There are washrooms at this park and a large grassy area for picnicking, where we stopped to have lunch. The parks are under the supervision of the Hamilton Conservation Authority.

On leaving the park, turn right on Ridge Road, cross over a cement bridge at the top of the Devil's Punch Bowl, pass a fruit stand and watch for a gravel pathway heading to the right, back into the forest. The trail will take you back to the original trail that you came in on and requires some hiking ability. Soon you will reach the main Bruce Trail. Turn left and continue toward the railway that you originally crossed over.

Cross the tracks again, turn left and find the path back into the forest on your right. This will take you back to the parking lot at Battlefield Park. The loop is about 3.2 km (2 mi.), and took us about two hours.

Remember, hiking is not a race. Be safety conscious on these trails, stop and examine the terrain, the beauty of nature, leave footprints, and only take photographs. Be sure you have food and plenty of water with you on any hike and dress in layered clothing in cool weather. You will warm up as you get into the hike, so taking off that extra sweater or jacket is a nice relief.

29
River and Ruin/Bruce Trail Link:

Difficulty: Beginner/Intermediate (hard packed earth, tree roots, some climbing)
Directions: From Hwy. 5 (Dundas St.) in Burlington, take Cedar Springs Rd. north about 10 minutes. Turn right (east) on Britannia Rd. to Blind Line. There is no admission and the only parking is a couple of turn-off areas at the stop signs on Britannia Road and Blind Line. Each could accommodate about two vehicles.

    The River and Ruin is a side link of the Bruce Trail, and is located east of Cedar Springs Road north of the city of Burlington. It is about 3.2 km. (2 mi.) loop and took us about two hours and thirty minutes to complete, because of our heightened curiosity and the need to explore every nook and cranny. We shot two rolls of film, and joked about what we would do if we encountered Big Foot. It was overcast and a few raindrops were starting to fall, giving a dark, eerie look to the trail. I wasn't with my usual hiking partner (my husband), but instead had taken my daughter along on our first hike, together. Two women with wonderful imaginations on a dark, deserted trail was a little unnerving, and at one point, we both decided to stop telling scary stories. We were getting a little jumpy.

    As we started the loop off the main Bruce Trail down into the valley, I had just finished telling a True Crime story I had seen on television, about a mother whose daughter had been missing for two years when the police decided to reopen the file. A new search party had been formed and the mother wanted to tag along. As she walked along a ditch she noticed something white under some shrubbery. It turned out to be her daughter's skull. Just as we were saying how awful that would be, I noticed something perfectly round and pure white under a bush. It could not have happened at a worse moment. I put my arms out and we both stopped dead in our tracks. "What's that?" I whispered. It looked like a piece of Styrofoam, the size of a human skull. Slowly, I walked over to it and touch it with my foot. It felt like Styrofoam, but it seemed to be attached to the ground. I gave it another nudge and it gave a little "pop" and tipped over. It was the biggest mushroom, we had ever seen!

We looked around, and on the other side of the trail there were more. Some in clusters, others off by themselves, all perfectly round and white. They all consisted of a form of fungi or mushroom-type growth, with one single stem or stock growing out of the ground. We could hardly believe our own eyes, so in the event that no one else would believe our findings, I made sure I had some photos, just for the record. Farther along the trail stood the stone ruins of an old house, almost hidden from the trail by overgrown shrubs and five-foot weeds. Luckily my daughter, a few feet behind me, looked back and shouted, "What is that?" By this time we were thoroughly spooked and I froze. "What is what?" I asked, almost afraid to look. I turned expecting to see something big and hairy coming out of the woods, but instead there stood the picturesque ruins of the old house.

We gingerly made our way through the weeds, until we were close enough to reach out and feel the texture of the stone constructed walls. Only three of the walls remained standing, the fourth had long since fallen into the bowels of the basement. Old wooden beams above the door openings were still preserved as perfectly as the day they were placed there. Axe markings were clearly gouged, as each beam had been honed into rectangles for supporting beams. We took numerous photographs as we peered into the gapping cavern. Through the window openings we tried to imagine the history, and who might have lived there.

We got back on the trail and found wildflowers still in bloom, even in the first week of October, and although there was a cool breeze, the warmth of the sun filtered through the trees. Soon we came to Bronte Creek, and just beyond where the blue markings of the Bruce Trail link ended, was a large cement bridge. We took some photos and retraced our steps back to the loop trail, turned right and followed along the Creek.

Enormous willow trees, hundreds of years old, created an unusual landscape. Some had fallen and were twisted in weird forms under their weight, while others were relying on the support of other trees. One of these trees had fallen right at the banks of the creek, creating a picture perfect place to stop for lunch. My daughter found a comfortable seat in the branches of a small tree, gently relaxed, crossed her arms and asked what was for lunch. Since tuna sandwiches were the only item on the menu, she said they were the best she had ever eaten. Any sandwich would have tasted like a gourmet meal, when accompanied by the sounds of a babbling brook and a whispering autumn breeze.

Right at the end of the River and Ruin Side Trail, where the familiar blue T-shaped markings indicated we had reach the end of the loop, was another bridge over the creek, constructed entirely of steel mesh. We took more photographs and returned to the main trail to complete our round trip. Farther along, we began to ascend out of the valley. The steep, rocky climb was the most difficult part of the trail, but we made it back.

We still held the excitement and thrill of the hike, and felt an enormous feeling of accomplishment. It was a fun-filled mother and daughter day.

30
Webster's Falls at Greensville:

Difficulty: Beginner (some climbing)
Directions: Take Hwy. 8 north from Dundas, turn right on Brock Road and right at the flashing light onto Harvest Road. Watch closely, and turn right on Short Road and left onto Fallsview Road. This parking lot is close to Webster's Falls and the picnic area. Farther down Harvest Road is the second parking lot for Tews Falls and Dundas Peak Lookout. No admission fees.

Webster's Falls in spring is Niagara in miniature, but with the added autumn colours, it brings new life and beauty to this spectacular natural wonder. The thunder of water can be heard long before you're standing at the crest.

You can safely view the falls from many angles, and if you are more adventurous, a long narrow stairway leads down to the very base of the falls. Whether you are looking up at the falls or down, or prefer a panoramic view from a distance, you won't be disappointed viewing these falls any time of the year.

In summer, you could plan to spend the whole day picnicking, exploring, or hiking the Bruce Trail that leads through the park and along the rim of the gorge. This area is large, with picnic tables, barbeques, gazebo and the added attraction of the fast- flowing Spencer Creek, which runs along the park to the brink of the falls, then tumbles violently to the depths below.

The stairs down to the base of the falls are narrow and can be extremely dangerous in winter or slippery when wet. In October, we descended the stairway,

Webster's Falls

where large flat rocks provided a picturesque spot to enjoy our lunch. The stairs leading to the base of the falls are all that remains of a powerhouse that burned many years ago, and was never replaced. In the 1800's, many mills sprang up along the creek with the availability of water power.

On leaving the falls, go back up the stairs and follow the trail that continues over a cobblestone bridge. It then enters the woods along a gorgeous stretch of the Bruce Trail, where it meanders along the edge of the gorge. Gravestones moved from the original burial grounds have been incorporated into a memorial site, located along the trail. This memorial site was established for members of the Webster family, who were landowners here, back in the 1800's.

Following the Bruce Trail along the escarpment, you'll find a number of stairways and some moderate uphill climbing. This will lead to another parking lot, where the main Bruce Trail continues on to Tews Falls. To reach the lookout over Tews Falls, there are also a number of stairways, but it is well worth the climb when you peer down into the dark depths.

Although Tews Falls, at 41 metres in height, is higher than Webster's Fall, it has very little water flowing over its crest. The size of the spectacular view gives an indication of the volume of water that must have been present thousands of years ago, when the deep, bowl-shaped gorge was originally formed.

The trail clings to the edge of the rocky cliffs and here you can pick up the side trail that forms a loop, taking you out to the Dundas Peak and a spectacular view of Dundas Valley. You can return on the same trail, or turn to your left and follow the trail that loops back through the woods, to the parking lot on Harvest Rd. If you are parked at Webster's Falls, the return trip would take approximately two hours.

31

Borer's Falls/Bruce Trail Side Trail:

Difficulty: Intermediate/Advanced (some climbing and steep uphill grades)
Directions: From Hwy. 403, take Hwy. 6 North. At the flashing light intersection, turn left (west), on York Road. Travel about 2.3 km and watch for a stone utility building on the right. The parking lot is just to the west of it, with a wooden sign indicating the Borer's Falls Trail. After parking, walk west along the grassy area until you see the trail going into the woods on your right, with blue rectangles indicating the Bruce Side Trail to the falls. No admission fee.

Although autumn is not my favourite time of year, I have to admit that it really is the best time to take a hike. Mid-October, with the bright sunshine, cool breeze and the absence of those pesky bugs, provides all the elements needed to experience nature and get some exercise. This is the time when you should start dressing in layers, as you will increase your body heat as you get farther along into your hike. Whatever season it is, make sure you have plenty of water.

The Bruce Side Trail to Borer's Falls is only about a 4 km. (1.5 miles) round trip, but on the way to Borer's Falls the trail is almost entirely up hill. The path was a little muddy from the rain the day before, but with hard packed earth, tree roots and rocks, it was not difficult to get good footing.

Some leaves had already fallen, and nuts and wild pears were scattered about the landscape. Like all hiking trails, the excitement of discovery is what I find so fascinating, and no two trails are ever the same.

There is always something new to be discovered and this trail was no exception. Soon, the side trail marked with a 'T' of blue rectangles ended, and we arrived at the main Bruce Trail marked in white. There is no sign here pointing the way to the falls, but turn to your left and follow the trail. We experienced, for the first time, a chain securely attached to a tree, to aid in climbing a steep section of rock that only had a few toeholds to secure you from slipping. Leather climbing gloves would have been useful here. This brought us up to a relatively flat surface, and the trail that lead along the edge of the escarpment to a bench lookout.

The fall colours were just beginning to form in all their glory and from that vantage point, looking down into the valley, it was like being on top of the world. Squirrels and chipmunks are familiar sights, but the trees and fallen logs, rock formations and scenic outlooks are always different.

Even if the trail is difficult and you must be aware of where you are placing your feet, make sure to stop and take a look around. You might miss something that you may never see again, on any other trail. I find it a little sad that these trails are virtually deserted. For those of you who have never taken a hike, you are missing a world that some of us have forgotten. For me, it brings back childhood memories of living in the country and of valuable things learned about nature. Sometimes the quietness gives us an overwhelming feeling of being the only people on earth.

Before starting your hike, it is always nice to have a specific destination, and the anticipation of arriving there adds to the enjoyment of the trip. On this trail, Borer's Falls held my curiosity and interest. We had just had a full day of rain, so I was hoping for a large volume of water. Early spring is usually the best time to view waterfalls, but I was still hoping.

Borer's Falls is 16 m (52 ft) in height. The width at the top is approximately 9 m (29 ft.). Borer's Creek that feeds the falls is small, and doesn't provide a large volume of water, but you know at one time it must have been huge, in order to create such a deep gorge below. This valley runs into the conservation area and the woodlands of the Royal Botanical Gardens.

Years ago, the water tumbling over the falls provided enough power to operate a saw mill, owned by the Borer family for over a century. This mill was large enough to provide work and support for the entire village of Rock Chapel. But today the water flowing over this ribbon falls gave only a preview of what might have been. I was not disappointed, for any waterfall, big or small, always fascinates me, and being able to get close enough to hear the water babbling along the creek and then tumbling over the edge creating a foggy spray below, was well worth the hike. I wanted to get to the bottom of the falls to take photographs looking up, but the gorge is extremely dangerous, with no access trail. It is an easy walk through groves of lilacs to get to the crest of the falls.

In May, this area would be a picturesque setting, with a heavenly smell. If you happen to see clumps of lilacs bushes along any of the trails, it is a sure sign that the place where you are standing had been, many years ago, a pioneer homestead.

On our return trip, we stopped at the bench lookout and ate our lunch. Even though the sun still held some warmth, the cool breeze kept us from staying too long, so I took one more photograph and we began our hike back down into the valley. Going down-hill exercises a whole new set of muscles, specifically the top of your thighs, as I discovered the following day. In about two hours, we were back at the parking lot. The trail to Borer's Falls is a short hike, but full of sights, sounds and smells of autumn.

32

Ball's Falls/ Twenty Mile Creek:

Difficulty: Beginner
Directions: From the Burlington Skyway Bridge, QEW Niagara bound, exit 57 (Vineland). It will take about 20 minutes. Head into Vineland and turn left on Victoria Ave., pass over King St. and watch for sign for Ball's Falls. Honorary admission fee.

No matter how many times I visit the Niagara Escarpment, I'm always amazed at the incredible rock formations and breathtaking scenery.

We've never been disappointed and marvel at the feeling of peace and accomplishment after a hike. At times what you imagine you'll see is far from the truth. What was initially a disappointment for us the first week in November, became an unusual experience.

There is an upper and lower Ball's Falls, which is fed by the Twenty Mile Creek. To view the upper falls, cross a wooden bridge located near the large parking lot, turn to your left and follow along the banks of the creek. In a few minutes, you will find yourself on a trail leading into the forest, which seems to be cut away from the overhanging rocks of the escarpment. It is a good walking trail for beginners and children, since safety precautions such as chain link fencing and rock walls have been installed near the escarpment edge. Many times, when you are focused on the incredible beauty of the trail ahead of you, you forget to look up, but that could be a mistake.

Overhead on this trail are bold rock formations, which, coupled with the autumn colours, comprised a photographer's retreat. Many of the leaves had fallen, covering the path, but as we scuffed through them, a nutty aroma penetrated our nostrils. It was a perfect fall day to take a hike. It was cold and overcast, but a calm breeze made it feel much warmer than it really was. In anticipation of seeing the upper falls, I kept listening for the sound of cascading water, but heard nothing. At first, I thought that was odd, but decided that perhaps we were still just too far away.

Within 20 minutes, down an embankment to the left of the path, we came upon stone ruins. According to the historical plaque mounted there, it was the remnants of a wool mill built in 1824, by George Ball. Water from the falls created the power to run the mill, which produced woollen cloths and yarn. By today's appearance of the ruins, it seems to have been a small structure, but the historical photograph shows it was a very large building, five stories high, and was thought to have housed eight weaving looms. In 1830, several houses with a large boarding house were constructed to provide living accommodations for the workers. By 1851, the wool mill employed 30 workers.

A few yards away, we noticed a chain link fence and stonewall. I rushed to the edge, camera at the ready, to get my first view of the upper falls. I could not believe it! There was not a drop of water falling over the edge, only a large gaping hole, where water normally falls 11 m (36 ft.). On checking with the checked with the Niagara Peninsula Conservation Authority, I was advised it is very rare that the falls dry up completely, even though dry summers will lessen the volume of water.

We ventured out onto the creek bed and walked across large flat rocks, dried and bleached white by the sun. Patches of algae and weeds lay crisp and brittle, barely identifiable in the crevices of the rock. It was fascinating and a little spooky to be able to stand where, in spring and summer, torrents of raging water flowed over this very spot. Layers of rock could be seen forming a horseshoe shape all the way to the gorge below. Along the top edge near the lookout, groves of lilac bushes promised a display of fragrance and beauty, when spring arrives next year. Although we were disappointed as we left and returned on the same trail to view the lower falls, it reminded us that our summer had been extremely hot and dry, with very little rainfall to nourish the creeks. Fifty species of migrant and nesting birds are often seen here and on our return trip from the upper falls, we noticed a Downy Woodpecker flitting from branch to branch, taking little notice of our presence.

To view the lower falls, cross the paved road you drove in on, and you can't miss it. No water in the upper falls meant no water in the lower falls, but in its absence you could get the full impact of the layers of rock and formations that would be normally hidden. It was a fantastic view, peering into the gorge at a depth of 27 m (88 ft).

In this area, an historical village nestles just above the falls, with small log homes, a white church that can be rented for weddings, a large barn, other fascinating structures, and washrooms, which were all closed for the season. If you want to be introduced to the Niagara Escarpment, this is the place to begin. The trail is short and easily walked.

The path to the upper falls is the longest and would take about 20 minutes, one-way. This is a 567-hectare historical park and conservation area, with access to the Bruce Trail, and is available for group camping for youth groups, service clubs, and conservation groups, only.

During the winter months, it's open to snow-shoeing and cross-country skiing. The regular season is from April – November from 8:00 am to 8:00 pm.

The view from Mount Nemo

33
Mount Nemo Trails:

DIFFICULTY: Beginner/Intermediate (hard packed earth, rock, and tree roots)
DIRECTIONS: From Hwy. 401, at Burlington, take Guelph Line South (exit 312), turn east on Colling Rd. to the park entrance. From the QEW, take Guelph Line North (exit 102), turn east at Colling Rd. to the park entrance. There is an admission fee.

The sun was shining and the crispness of the air carried a nutty smell, as we scuffed through the leaves on the trail leading to the main lookout.

It is an easy walk, wheelchair accessible, and takes approximately 20 minutes. The breathtaking view at the lookout is well worth the walk. Standing 968 feet above sea level, spread out before you is 31 miles of farmland, a golf course, and tiny ribbons of highway. On most days, the communities of Milton, Brampton and Toronto, along with Rattlesnake Point can be seen on the horizon. There are benches if you want to just spend some time enjoying the view, or taking a few minutes to rest from the short hike.

From that central point, you can choose from two trail loops. We took the north loop first, and hiked right along the edge of the escarpment, braving the gale-forced winds that had sprung up. It was a relatively warm day for the first week in November, but the strong wind made it much cooler.

Along this trail there are rocks covered in patches of bright green moss, twisted tree roots, deep caverns, and at that time of year, fallen leaves that made the rocks extra slippery, unless you were wearing proper hiking boots. All along were areas where you could again look over the edge of the escarpment, and take in another angle of the countryside below. Unusual tree formations were particularly interesting, as they twisted and curved, seeming to struggle to find some nourishment to grow against the rock, forcing their roots to search aimlessly for some earth to provide a base for their adult growth.

As you reach the trail's end on the escarpment, the path turns to the left, and leads you into an easy walk through the trees, back to the Brock Harris Lookout, where you began. That loop took about an hour, stopping for pictures and taking in the view.

From the lookout, if you still have energy left, you can take the south loop, which is a little easier walking, and gives you again, another angle of the valley below. On our hike that day, we came across professional climbers, who had just tied off and were guiding themselves over the edge of the cliff. I looked down to where they were going and my stomach took a little flip. Hanging over the edge, with his head at my feet level, preparing to descend, the leader said he'd be descending a "short climb," of about 500 feet. He explained that after they reached the bottom, they would climb back up. His group had climbed cliffs down through the United States, and around Ottawa, Ontario. I just wished him luck and we continued on our much safer journey around the south loop.

By this time we were getting hungry, so we picked a couple of large rocks very near the edge, with some small trees to keep us secure in case we needed a hand hold. I nestled in on the rock farthest out, took off my backpack, looked out across the valley and then realized how close I was to the edge. To my husband's surprise, he couldn't believe that I had chosen that rock with my fear of heights. I guess watching those cliff climbers, I felt brave attaching myself to that rock, on level ground.

All the people we met were kind and friendly. Some were walking dogs, some with children, and all visibly enjoying the walk in the fresh autumn air.

The south loop is a more relaxed walk along the escarpment edge, and turns to the right toward an open meadow, a narrow forest trail and a quarry site. The south loop also takes about an hour, and soon you are on the trail heading back to the parking lot.

At certain times, turkey vultures have been seen gliding in the updrafts of the cliffs. Looking down on them, instead of up, is a unique turn of events.

These trails give you spectacular vistas, some cardio exercise (a stress reliever), and the wonderful feeling of getting back in touch with nature.

34
Twenty-Mile Creek:

Difficulty: Advanced
Directions: From the QEW Niagara bound, take exit 57 into Vineland. Turn left on Victoria Ave., and left onto King St. (Hwy. 8). Follow this until you see the town sign for Jordan. On your left is the Butterball Restaurant and the parking lot to begin the trail. There is no admission fee. Washrooms are located at the restaurant or at Ball's Falls.

For those of you who are experienced hikers and are looking for a challenge, this trail is the one for you. It not only tests your physical abilities, it also rewards you at the end for all your efforts, with a natural wonder of historical interest.

It begins on Highway 8 (King St.) at the sign for the town of Jordan. There is a small restaurant on your left, called the Butterball. Turn into the parking lot, and on your left, behind the restaurant property, you will clearly see the path leading off along the banks of the creek. The trail meanders along the edge of the restaurant property, and then takes you down stone steps to a cement tunnel underpass. The trail markings are blue circles, but there are not many and they're difficult to follow. But you cannot get lost, as long as you follow along the creek.

The trail is very rocky and provides a challenge every step of the way. Yet, the overwhelming beauty lulls you into thinking you've left the modern world and have escaped into a natural paradise. It was November and leaves had covered a large portion of the trail, which made walking on rock slippery while hiding cracks and crevices. This is the time, when you rely on your hiking boots for grip and ankle support.

With green leaves still attached to the trees, a carpet of gold leaves and moss clinging to the enormous rocks, it was like entering various outdoor rooms that nature had meticulously landscaped. I never get over the beauty of the escarpment trails. You would think that after hiking so many they would all begin to look the same, but that's far from the truth.

All along this trail you can see the Twenty Mile Creek, although at this time of year it was dry. The huge rocks were clearly visible on the creek bed, some worn smooth by the flow of swift water during spring and summer. At times, when you looked ahead, it seemed the trail disappeared, but it was easily found as it cut through hills and valleys, loose rock, tree roots, and fallen logs. Hiking difficult trails may tempt you to focus only on where you're placing your feet, but if you don't stop and look around, you may end up missing something unusual, or that perfect photograph.

By now you are very close to the edge of the creek, but just as you think the trail is becoming easier to navigate, there are a number of steep steps taking you about one-third of the way up the escarpment. At the top, there is a platform with built-in benches. You may want to take a breather here, and look down on what you have just come through. From the platform, turn to your right and you'll come to an intersection. Keep following the path to the right. This is where the Bruce Trail merges with the trail you're following.

You never lose sight of the creek anywhere along this path. In spring, when there's a lot of water, it must be an unforgettable experience. As you hike along this trail, look up to your left and see the edge of the escarpment far above. At some point you know that the climb to the top is somewhere ahead of you.

About a mile (1.6 km) into your hike, you will come to a long, steep set of stairs. These are very rugged, and carved out of the face of the slope, with only a rope serving as a railing. The steps are far apart (I call them steps for tall people) and consist of hard packed earth and wood. Perhaps, with a stop or two to catch your breath, you will eventually find yourself at the very top of the escarpment, with a bird's eye view of the valley below.

Turn to your right, following the escarpment edge and just when you think you have scaled the worst, ahead is another set of stairs. But this is your payoff. The steps are well built and easy walking, and at the bottom you will come to a clearing, located right at the edge of the historical village at Ball's Falls. Here you can enjoy a picnic, view the upper and lower falls, and explore the historical buildings between April and November.

If you have parked at the restaurant, the return trip is no less exciting. Everything appears different from another direction. The round trip is about 3 mi (4.9 km). Spring would be the best time to view the falls and the Twenty Mile Creek.

35

Felker's Falls on Red Hill Creek:

Difficulty: Beginner (wheelchair accessible)
Directions: QEW Niagara, exit 88 (Stoney Creek). Right on Centennial Parkway up the escarpment. Right on Mud Street, right on Paramount Drive and right on Ackland St. to Felker's Falls Conservation Area. There are no washrooms and no admission fees.

Did you ever look out the window and know in your heart that you really must get some exercise and go for a walk? But then, you start making excuses. It is too cold, too hot, too windy, or it looks like rain. I have done it, so don't think you are alone, but the trick is to dress for the weather and get out there.

This hike should not be missed by anyone, so bundle the kids, put the dog on a leash, find a friend or family member who is disabled but using a wheelchair, walker, or an electric scooter, and get them out too for a day of exploration. It won't take a lot of time and the experience will not be forgotten.

This trail is surprisingly located right in the middle of a residential area, and when you follow my directions, you will think that I have gotten you lost. There is a large wooden conservation sign that you cannot miss. At the beginning of the trail is a plaque dedicating the trail to Peter Street, where it is noted that he was disabled and in his lifetime, inspired the disabled and others to have a zest for life. It is a short hike, about one mile, (1.7 km), but within that short distance, we found the best that any trail could offer. The trail is extra wide and consists of hard packed stone dust. It follows a rail fence rimming the gorge.

In a short distance, you'll get your first glimpse of Felker's Falls and a breathtaking view of the gorge. The water drops about 70 ft. (21.5 m) to the Red Hill Creek below. We had had an extremely dry summer, but even with a low volume of water flowing over the crest, it still provided a surprisingly great show.

I recommend spring and fall as the best times to view the falls and gorge as leaves are not obstructing your view. In spring the volume of water would be at its peak. We were there mid-November, on a windy, warm day, when most of the leaves had fallen, laying a golden carpet on the forest floor. Under the leaves, remnants of wild flower plants lay partially hidden, bedding down for their long winter sleep.

There are numerous lookout areas throughout the park, complete with benches for eating lunch, or just taking a rest. The rail fencing that follows the rim of the gorge is constructed so that it does not obstruct the view from a wheelchair. The trail follows the edge of the escarpment in a loop, but there are two other trails that cross the forest within that loop.

All of these paths take you out to the main trail. If you'd like to continue on the other side of the gorge, follow the Bruce Trail about a quarter of a mile. Look for a small white sign to the right of the parking lot for the trail. There is a steel bridge over the creek, a slight incline with rocks that serve as good footing, and a narrow path that follows the opposite rim of the gorge. From here, the breathtaking view of the falls was truly overwhelming, and I couldn't get enough. It was like a picture postcard. This part of the Bruce Trail is easily navigated, proven by an elderly couple we met that had easily found their way to this magical spot.

This trail, though short, is one of the most interesting and pleasant of all the hikes I have profiled. I think this hike excited me the most because of its accessibility to everyone – so no excuses.

To close off our hiking book – here's some top trails:
FAY'S FIVE FAVOURITES:

Tiffany Falls and Sherman Falls (pp 40-43)
Both are spectacular, and the hiking is challenging.

Crawford Lake and the Bruce Trail across the Nassagawaya Canyon (pp 44-47)
This hike will test your physical endurance, and provide a day full of exciting exploration.

Beamer Trail/ side link to Bruce Trail (pp 25-28)
Beamer Falls and the Forty Mile Creek is a magnificent sight in springtime, with its spellbinding vista of raging water, and thundering waterfalls.

The Devil's Punch Bowl (pp 102-105)
The trail to the top is steep, but to be able to look down into this unusual circular bowl formation, created millions of years ago, is well worth the hike.

The Black Creek Side Trail (pp 99-101)
A narrow opening in the rock face called "The Hole in the Wall" proved to be an exciting surprise and the highlight of the hike.

The above are my favourites. They may be your favourites as well – or you may have others. But the important thing is to get out and enjoy nature.

Dress for the weather and Take a Hike. You'll be amazed at the feeling of freedom and accomplishment you derive exploring the amazing beauty of nature.

- Fay Beck-Ryall.

Manor House Publishing
(905) 648-2193